MW00873078

BUSINESS BOOKS AREN'T FUNNY

The Living Hell of Starting a Business and the Relentless Arrogance and Endurance Required to Make it to the Finish Line. Good Luck.

BRYAN MESSMER

Cover Design by Pixel Studios

Edited by Kathryn F. Galán, Wynnpix Productions

DISCLAIMER: Anything written in this book is not representative of any statements of fact. Bryan Messmer is not an expert on anything and most people tend to be surprised to find out he can read, let alone write an entire book. This is a book written purely for entertainment purposes.

PRINT ISBN 978-1-7291-3297-5

To Mur, the best bad dog I could have ever asked for

CONTENTS

INTRODUCTION: THIS IS A BOOK ON HOW TO SURVIVE OPENING A BUSINESS 7

CHAPTER 1: THE LEAST ROMANTIC THING YOU'RE EVER GOING TO DO 10

CHAPTER 2: AN IN-BETWEEN PROJECT THAT JUST KINDA GOT AWAY FROM ME 19

CHAPTER 3: SO YOU'RE AN ENTREPRENEUR AND YOU TELL PEOPLE THAT? 28

CHAPTER 4: YOU MAKE YOUR OWN LUCK? 38

CHAPTER 5: "JUST BECAUSE YOU HAVE A BIG DREAM AND FOUR THOUSAND DOLLARS IN YOUR BANK ACCOUNT DOESN'T MEAN YOU DESERVE SHIT" 48

CHAPTER 6: BEAUTIFUL DENVER, COLORADO 58

CHAPTER 7: READ THE RIGHT BOOKS 66

CHAPTER 8: GOOD PEOPLE CAN STILL GIVE BAD ADVICE 71

CHAPTER 9: MOVING A MOUNTAIN ONE SLAB OF CONCRETE AT A TIME 80

CHAPTER 10: WHO YOU ARE ACCOUNTABLE TO WILL MAKE A BIG DIFFERENCE 86

CHAPTER 11: BLUE RIBBON IN 1970-SOMETHING 92

CHAPTER 12: YOU DON'T KNOW WHAT YOU DON'T KNOW 95

CHAPTER 13: IT'S LIKE THE TIME THEY KILLED MY BROTHER ... 99

CHAPTER 14: DOING SOMETHING FOR THE SAKE OF DOING IT 106

CHAPTER 15: HOW MANY *NOS* ARE LEFT IN THE NO BANK? 111

CHAPTER 16: OTHER PEOPLES' SUGGESTIONS 122

CHAPTER 17: WHAT'S YOUR UNFAIR ADVANTAGE? 131

CHAPTER 18: THIS BOOK WAS WRITTEN IN 40 DAYS 137

CHAPTER 19: CULTURE 139

CHAPTER 20: THE THING WE BUILT AND IT'S HERE 142

CHAPTER 21: BORN OUT OF NECESSITY 147

CHAPTER 22: SOMETIMES THAT NINE-TO-FIVE LOOKS PRETTY
    SWEET 155

CHAPTER 23: WHAT IF IT WAS EASY? 162

CHAPTER 24: STAYING HONEST WITH EVERYONE 170

CHAPTER 25: DO NOT DAYDREAM 174

CHAPTER 1: IT'S NEVER FINISHED 176

APPENDIX: BRYAN'S FAVORITE BOOKS 178

THANK YOU 179

ABOUT BRYAN 180

INTRODUCTION

THIS IS A BOOK ON HOW TO SURVIVE OPENING A BUSINESS

AFTER BEING KICKED in the nuts about one hundred and fifty times by the City of Denver, I realized something: this isn't so bad. I haven't built an empire, but, at the time of this writing, I am eight months into yet another business, and this time feels different.

If you're reading the introduction, then you're a better person than I am. I wrote this book to help folks remember they're not alone when they're hanging on by a thread and everything seems impossible. To let you know you're likely not the first person to go through the misery of starting a business. Even if your business is insanely unusual, it's still a business, and it can get done, if you are willing to grind it out and not quit!

There are so many obstacles in the way of building something. Not all obstacles are tangible, like a truck blocking the road. In fact, most of the obstacles manifest in obscure and seemingly unnecessary ways.

It will seem, at times, *"this only happens to me"* is the feeling you wake up with and go to sleep with for days. But that's just it, though: it doesn't *just* happen to you. You are not special. The bullshit that comes with building, starting, or creating something happens to all of us. If you are able to take every tangible and intangible "NO" and keep going, then you've got a shot at getting to the end. But you are not special.

Everyone will use the phrase *blood, sweat, and tears,* but it's literal, in some cases. Most cases. When I thought I'd broken my knuckle after a block of concrete smashed my hand between a wall and the slab, I bled. When I tried to truthfully explain my PFS (personal financial statement) to the underwriters, I was sweating. And when I finally received the Certificate of Occupancy, I think I cried.

No matter what anyone tells you, you *can*, but it's going to start by everyone telling you, you *can't*.

Why it's Worth Reading

This is definitely not worth reading if you have more important parts of your project to handle. Do not use this book to procrastinate. And this is not a step-by-step recipe for opening a business. I am far from being an expert in anything.

But experiences worth sharing can make a massive difference when you are going through it. And when I say *it,* I'm referring to the living hell of opening a business.

Not every chapter will be applicable to each reader's circumstances at the time of reading this; in fact hopefully, for your sake, there won't be more than a couple chapters that are relevant to what's occurring for you at any one time. More than that would be a perfect storm of problems, and you would need way more than *this* book to get you through. (But you'll need more than this or any book, for that matter, to open a business or build anything).

My hope is you will find something in each chapter that will boost the "NOs" in your NO Bank and help you to really endure. (*NO Bank will be explained later.)

So, skim this book, rip it up, give it to a friend, leave it on the shelf, or recycle it, but try to get something out of it. Something to get you through the hard times that inevitably lie ahead for anyone starting or setting up a new business.

CHAPTER 1

THE LEAST ROMANTIC THING YOU'RE EVER GOING TO DO

Start-ups and Spouses: the other day we had a mouse in the house, and I told my wife I was starting a cat rental business.

EVEN IF YOU'RE SINGLE now, you should still read this chapter. Possibly one of the most important aspects, if not *the* most important aspect of starting your own business is the people currently in your life.

It is not romantic to start a business, and it is not romantic to fail at starting a business. There are few things that will make your spouse *unhorny* faster than losing all your combined money.

The romcoms all lie. You think you're all going to be laughing it up and riding tandem bicycles through Central

Park after your organic juicing business dies on the table because it has innumerable competitors and because your food cost, labor, and rent are out of control?

Now, you're never home, and even when you do come home, you have to hear, "More juice?" So, you start adding a little rum to your banana drinks and then a little more, and now you're sad, alone, drunk, and soon-to-be broke.

Some exceptionally prosperous people will tell you, in order to launch successfully, you will have to eat, breathe, sleep, and sleep with your business idea to even give it a chance at becoming a successful endeavor, venture, thing, or whatever.

But what if you're already married?

Great question. The answer is to get divorced immediately. And if you have a girlfriend or boyfriend (unless their parents are wealthy... More on *that* in Chapter 3), then the best thing to do is break up with them, even if it hurts.

No! This is actually the worst idea—almost as bad as simply expressing to them they are less important to you than the success of your business. A person who loves you will believe in you. And it is critically important to *appreciate* them throughout the grueling process of building and launching a business. Yes, there will be times when they are annoying as shit, but guess what? You're going to be way worse to live with than they are.

When you're going on and on about how brutal everything is, trying to get permits, close on the loan, or deal with a horrible sonofabitch of an engineer, all you're *really* doing is ear-fucking the shit out of a person who loves and believes in you the most. You're expecting them to just listen because they're supposed to? They did and they didn't sign up for this. When they decided to bed down with a *"go-getter"/entrepreneur*, they may or may not have known what they were really signing up for.

When you're already married and just starting a business, remember: you are not rolling the dice only on your security and future, but on that of your partner's, as well. Even if they absolutely knew what they were getting themselves into (and, realistically, they definitely didn't), it is still the dreamer's responsibility to be aware and considerate of the other person's stress. Never say or think you're "doing *allll* of this" for them, because you're really not. Hopefully, you have an excellent reason for creating whatever it is you're creating, but please, pull your head out, if you think you're doing it for *them*.

Your wonderful, beautiful, supportive person is down for the ride because they love you. Don't forget that.

If you're not married or in love, then Mark Cuban will tell you that you have no time for relationships when starting a business. And I would agree. But businesses are not only built by sad and lonely people. To clarify this point, what Mark and I are both saying isn't that you can't enjoy the company of others, but it is doubtful you are going to be able to adequately dedicate the time required to create a successful relationship *and* be able to give your new business the attention and dedication required to effectively build that business into something successful. When you're stretched too thin, both things suffer.

It can get confusing fast when you *think* you're working your ass off for someone else. We quickly convince ourselves—over and over again, in fact—we are working to benefit the ones we love the most.

Think of your goals separately, personal versus professional. It's not a new concept by any means, but it is especially relevant in the Age of Entrepreneurialism.

By grinding constantly and putting in the early mornings combined with the late nights, your business will likely do well. But there is no doubt your personal relationships will suffer. Knowing what you want your life to look like and then writing it down is the most effective way to have a clear understanding with your spouse of what you're both working for. By all means, work the eighty-plus-hour weeks when you need to, but don't forget the other person in the equation and their sacrifice, as well.

Without getting too philosophical, what's the point?

When I launched Easy Float, my most recent business, it was literally the month after I'd gotten married. Now, I know what you're probably thinking, and the answer is, *yes*! I am still married to the same person as of today. What does it mean to go through all the planning, building, prelaunch stuff, permitting, and marketing of a business while being engaged? It means I didn't help with planning my own wedding at all!

Wow, what a catch? Right! Nope, I wasn't useful at all. However, I think this is an opportunity for a *takeaway* to come into the picture.

We were going to get married in the mountains at a lake house in Colorado, where we live, but when my wonderful fiancée began asking me about table cloths, DJs, chairs, lights, and hotels for our guests, I quickly realized this was not going to be cool. I love my wife, but there was no possible way I was down to plan a wedding. (I like to think I would've been more interested in being involved had I not been right in the middle of working on the launch of a brand-new business, but I am probably full of shit.)

Takeaway

✓ Hire yourself a Larry.

So, this could have gone a couple of different ways. Call off the wedding altogether, break my person's heart, and continue eating canned chili and drinking cruddy beer way too often. Or allow the business to fall by the wayside and get down on the tablecloth discussions. Or hire a travel agent named Larry and move the wedding to Mexico.

So that's what we did.

Now, it turned out Larry was a bit of a slippery character, but this just allowed me to take out some frustration on Larry rather than the love of my life. Is that healthy? Nope, not really.

But I had just paid a speeding ticket and was wearing my cowboy boots when I got a call from my fiancée telling me that Larry was making things difficult for her friend Jessica, so what the hell? Blow off some steam while on my way back down to the city building and permit office, where I'd have to take some more abuse from the ladies at the counter about having too many staples in my architectural drawings, all the while the meter maid is writing me yet another ticket? Sorry, Larry.

To be clear, though, I was still exposed to trick questions like, "Do you like seahorses or sand dollars better?" when my fiancée was doing save-the-dates. (And just so you know, this is a trick question: there is no right answer.) At the end of the day, we still got married, and it was excellent, and I am so grateful to have such an amazing person in my corner.

So that's it! We lived happily ever after, and the business opened, and I worked a reasonable number of hours and totally didn't neglect my brand-new marriage, and we went away on a sweet honeymoon, like normal fortunate Americans.... Wrong again, moosebreath.

After returning from a week in Mexico, which was been filled with unlimited tequila, sun, and new in-laws with whom I'd had countless small chats about how we were definitely going to visiting them just as soon as possible, we came back to Colorado, got officially married the next day, had a couple of scones and a coffee to celebrate, and I then immediately went back to work. Hundred-hours-plus weeks for the next five months. We didn't go on a honeymoon; rather, we tailgated in the parking lot of the new business with pizza and beers several nights per week.

Note on Balance: Even though your spouse is cool, they won't be cool for long, if you don't make a conscious effort to recognize them for how cool they are and for how cool your relationship is. Cool?

But what if your business partner *is* your spouse? Well then, you're an idiot.

No, not really. There are some incredible duos I have met who complement each other's style so well, they are incredibly successful. But can you imagine what it's like when it goes down? Relationships are work on their own, but add in the complex variable every day of the intricacies of building, owning, and operating a business with your soul mate—*that* is amazingly complicated.

Here's the key word from my subtitle: *endurance*. This is exactly what has to be kept in mind when the most illogical challenges arise, and they will arise. Separate the business dynamic from the love relationship, and take a massive step back to gain perspective, empathy, and patience. Don't let a dustup, especially if it's illogical, turn into a blowout; easier said than done, but attempt to catch yourself in the brief moment between action and reaction, in order to determine your response. Maybe the correct response is to let it go and endure.

To summarize what this chapter is all about and why it is so important: it's because the person in your life really didn't know what they signed up for, and you really do need them (not just for their credit score and health insurance). When you think things are getting rough for you, try to remember the ripple effect and what they might be going through. And always try to find a Larry to shout at before taking out frustrations on your life partner. The name of the game is endurance, and while you are reading stuff to understand that, they probably are not. You will wear them out quick if you're not careful, appreciative, and aware.

Chapter 1 Takeaways:

- ✓ They didn't know what they signed up for, so they, too, are going to have to endure
- ✓ Yell at Larry, not your soul mate... What about if Larry's your soul mate? No, that's not it.
- ✓ Any question about save-the-dates is a trick question

###

CHAPTER 2

AN IN-BETWEEN PROJECT THAT JUST KINDA GOT AWAY FROM ME

Your Crazy Idea

BELIEVE IT OR NOT, I didn't set out to build this business. I was in the process of selling some restaurants I had started with my brother, and it was kinda bittersweet, but timing is everything and it was time.

Starting something doesn't require you to know everything there is to know about it or even know how it ends. Too often, you find people reluctant to start because they feel they don't have enough answers yet. But how are you supposed to get the answers and the lessons without taking action and giving something a fair try?

I wouldn't suggest jumping in without at least doing *some* of the digging on what it is you're about take on before you really get into it, but think about the amount of information and experience you gain with, well, experience.

The crazy ideas are often the best, but it takes action. And the more you hear someone tell you it's crazy, the more you should think about actually pressing on *and then* actually pressing on. Just waiting to see if something works by sitting on the sidelines gives your competition too much of a head start. You've gotta take the crazy idea and get in the game. You'll figure out the other shit along the way.

I was halfway through the business plan for building a brewery when a friend from college told me about floating or sensory deprivation (salt water tanks to relax and reduce stress). I was working at a heavy metal brewery at night, making pizzas in order to learn everything I could about the brewing industry. Burgers by day, pizzas at night, and brewing beer whenever I had any free time. I know: it's amazing I am married.

But when Kevin told me about floating, I completely dismissed the idea. I was sure it was just another "Kevin" thing. Kevin is likely somewhere in the world right now, meditating to crystals, hammering back some Ayahuasca, and feeling chakras. Not judging, but definitely not my thing. Needless to say, I was a massive skeptic.

My first float was miserable: salt in my eyes; it was noisy, cold, and uncomfortable. But I still slept incredibly well that night. So I completely ate my words, which were, "I'm not doing that hippy bullshit."

I instantly went from massive skeptic to total believer because nothing I had attempted before for my chronic insomnia had made an impact like floating.

I began to peel back the layers on the float concept and couldn't believe the opportunity not only to create a unique and potentially very lucrative business, but to do something that could make a big difference for a lot of people searching for some avenue to alleviate and manage a variety of stresses and anxiety.

Here's where the fun started. I went from being, like, "Yeah, I have a couple restaurants" and people asking the name and about the menu to having to explain to people that, in my new job, I was opening a hippy bathtub center, 'cuz it can make people hallucinate and folks really seem to like that...

It is already an uphill battle to open any business. But when the business is something as fringe as flotation, you get a whole new set of challenges. An extensive buildout and a nice chunk of risk also come with about ninety percent of the population having no idea what the hell the thing is you're selling, let alone the potential benefits.

I figured I would purchase a few used tanks, lease a space, and pop open the doors to test the salty waters then just see how it went.

Now, I am certainly not the first person to open a weird business, and I am definitely not the first person to open a float center, but the *takeaways* from the experience taught me a number of things. Like how an "in-between" project can turn into something really excellent and exciting.

2 things:

- ✓ Don't let your lack of experience keep you from being open to unfamiliar opportunity.
- ✓ Just because something is harder to explain than burgers and beers, it still could be worth doing.

And here's where the endurance game comes into play. At its most basic explanation, building a business is as simple as how many times can you hear the word *NO* and keep going. When you have something you know people will want, but they just don't know it yet, there will be massive roadblocks all along the way. Even in building a "normal" business, you will encounter one thousand *NOs* along the way, so consider what it is like to develop a "weird" business.

Actually, think about Phil Knight.

Most people know who Phil Knight is: he is the founder of Nike. But a lot of folks don't realize that Phil's Nike was originally called Blue Ribbon, and before that, Phil described Nike as his "crazy idea." Doesn't seem that crazy now?

> *Nike, Inc. is the world's largest supplier and manufacturer of athletic shoes, apparel and other sports equipment. The company employed about 74,400 people worldwide in 2017, and their global revenue generated more than 34 billion U.S. dollars. The North American region of Nike generated the largest portion of the company's revenue that year; over 15 billion U.S. dollars, with the Oregon based company's athletic footwear segment generated approximately 9.7 billion U.S. dollars of that.*

> (www.statista.com/topics/1243/nike/)

When Phil told his dad, or anyone for that matter, that he wanted to import running shoes from Japan post-World War II, he would get the same reaction you would get, if you told people you were starting a salt-water tank center where people could relax and do nothing. Or if you told people you were starting an indoor swimming facility for dogs in Park City, Utah.

Angela

The Dog Dive in Park City is an excellent example of a business built on endurance. Underfunded, unfamiliar, and unusual, the Dog Dive has been open and thriving for more than two years now and has an excellent track record of providing incredible experiences for the pups and their people.

Angela is a good friend and former massage therapist who got sick of working on humans and made the leap to start her own business, focusing on man's best friend. With no guarantees of success, Angela took the risk, endured, and now is crushing it as a business owner while doing something she loves.

You might not be building the next Nike, but even if you're working on building a restaurant, you will still encounter the jackass who has to remind you the statistics on failing restaurants. It's another version of the word "*NO.*"

The doubters and the pessimist don't want you to keep going, even if it's on a subconscious level, and this likely only presents itself in an expression or tone of voice. Don't tear them down for their own insecurities, but definitely don't allow them to project their doubt on to you. In fact, if you have the ability to tastefully empathize, then you're a better person than I. These fuckers want to open a business, too, but they're too chicken shit to try because the sky is falling.

To quote Phil's mentor, partner, coach, and friend, Bill Bowerman, "The cowards never started, and the weak died along the way. That leaves us."

It's unnatural and uncomfortable to take off on a different and unsafe path. That's probably why most people don't do it. The post-industrial revolution conditioned most Americans to color inside the lines, but the entrepreneurial landscape in America drastically changed after the Great Recession, 2008. The safe bet wasn't so safe anymore, and a lot of millennials catch a lot of shit for not coloring inside the lines in response.

I'd like to avoid my soapbox of talking trash about the failed system and the baby boomers who are responsible, so I'll save that for another book. For now, let's try to agree that taking a risk comes with a lot of doubt, both from the outside and from within. But who cares?

My in-between project was meant to bridge me from restaurants to brewery, but here I am now, loving my business and writing a book. I look forward to hearing the questions, "Why would you write that?" and "You're writing a book??"

Every idea worth pursuing starts out as a crazy idea. Don't let the tones and facial expressions stop you. Smile and nod and think about the next thing you need to get done to keep your momentum.

The next thing you need to get done: compartmentalize the task/tasks ahead of you. That is the next thing you need to get done, and you will need to repeat the process several times throughout the journey. Focus is very challenging for the entrepreneur: they're typically very excitable and will be sincerely open to jumping in on the next venture without first considering the amount of work required to see it through.

By compartmentalizing the tasks in your project, you stand a much greater chance of making it all come together in the end. This is similar to why multitasking is stupid: you try to do too many things at once, and you end up half-assing a bunch of things. By taking the big, big end result and breaking it into more manageable parts, then it gets done.

If this seems too obvious to be in a book, it is. This is just another reminder, because entrepreneurs benefit from reminders.

Something practical:

- ✓ Stay organized from the very start. You'll thank yourself later. Rarely is there someone who actually flourishes in the chaos.
- ✓ Don't lie to yourself about the *method to the madness.* Keep your inbox tight.

###

CHAPTER 3

SO YOU'RE AN ENTREPRENEUR AND YOU TELL PEOPLE THAT?

Mindset/Mental Preparation

"If you want to understand the entrepreneur, study the juvenile delinquent. The delinquent is saying with his actions, 'This sucks. I'm going to do my own thing.'"

—Yvon Chouinard, American rock climber, environmentalist, and outdoor industry billionaire businessman. His company, Patagonia, is known for its environmental focus.

IT IS MY FIRM BELIEF that true entrepreneurs are never the self-described entrepreneur. You don't have time to stop and call yourself anything when you're working on a project you're passionate about and your back's against the wall.

Entrepreneurialism isn't a job, rather it's a mindset most successful entrepreneurs don't realize, because it isn't something they were required to cultivate. If you're reading this and thinking you want to become an entrepreneur, then stop thinking and you will have a much better chance of getting your shit done. The next thing you know, you will be describing what you *do* to a person at a party, and they will respond, "Oh, you're an entrepreneur!" This is the most satisfying way to find out. Putting *entrepreneur* as your job title on LinkedIn or in your dating profile just makes it seem like you're unemployed.

The entrepreneur concept connects closely with a few things, but for the sake of not making you read more ranting about how challenging it is to build something because it's hard and everyone thinks you're dumb and incapable, let's break it down into a couple of ideas or points or whatever:

- ✓ Mindset
- ✓ NO.
- ✓ And *Doing Something for the Sake of Doing it.*

The Mindset Factor

Lieutenant Commander (Ret.) Eric Potterat, Ph.D., a Naval Special Warfare Command psychologist, describes the

difference that separates elite athletes that win
championships and those that don't:

> *Physically, there's very little difference between*
> *athletes who win Olympic gold and the rest of the field.*
> *It's like the SEAL candidates we see here. Terrific*
> *hardware. Sit ups, pushups, running, swimming—off*
> *the charts, superhuman. But over at the Olympic center,*
> *the sports psychologists found that the difference*
> *between a medal and no medal is determined by an*
> *athlete's mental ability.*

https://navyseals.com/nsw/fear-and-mental-toughness/

Dr. Potterat has presented and related the critical
importance of mindset in the business world to organizations
interested in improving their teams and advancing their
success. The same mindset factor has to be applied from the
very beginning, if you are going to make it out on the other
side.

Going back to the self-described entrepreneur piece
mentioned earlier, this is simply not enough and is one
massive reason to avoid calling yourself an entrepreneur, in
the first place. Simply changing your title on LinkedIn is not
going to give you what you need to make something from
nothing, especially with the ever-mounting opposition of the
world around you.

I will say, if you are reading this, you are on the right side of the fence with regards to determining the required mindset to complete your crazy idea and achieve. I am definitely not saying that reading this book will make you the next Phil Knight, but, "leaders are readers," you're not just calling yourself the CEO. You're further cultivating the mindset that's required to survive the unsurmountable obstacles coming your way.

Look at the point made by Dr. Potterat, that the Navy SEALS are all super-humans with regards to the "hardware," but obviously not all of them can make it through the grueling BUDS experience. (If you're interested in learning more about BUDS and SEAL training, you should definitely check out some book suggestions in the appendix. But since I am not a SEAL and haven't studied the SEAL teams and culture to the appropriate extent, it isn't my place as a writer to get too in depth here.) The point I'm trying to make here is there are countless others out there just like you, who are interested in creating something or building a business. But what is going to be the difference between those who actually do it and those who just think about doing it or just kinda try? Your unfair advantage, or at least one of them, can be your unwillingness to accept the word *NO* as the failure of your pursuit. It sounds simple because it is. Simple, but not easy.

It's not easy because of the voice in your head.

Inner speech involvement in self-reflection was examined by reviewing 130 studies assessing brain activation during self-referential processing in key self-domains: agency, self-recognition, emotions, personality traits, autobiographical memory, and miscellaneous (e.g., prospection, judgments). The left inferior frontal gyrus (LIFG) has been shown to be reliably recruited during inner speech production. The percentage of studies reporting LIFG activity for each self-dimension was calculated. Fifty five percent of all studies reviewed indicated LIFG (and presumably inner speech) activity during self-reflection tasks; on average LIFG activation is observed 16% of the time during completion of non-self tasks (e.g., attention, perception)."

(https://www.ncbi.nlm.nih.gov/pmc/articles/PMC3462327/)

As if it isn't enough to have people and the universe (I know how that sounds) telling you *NO* and you can't do it, *now* you're going to have to overcome the inner doubter, too?

Yes, exactly.

As humans, we are wired to avoid risk in order to survive and continue to exist. When something is out of the ordinary, it garners attention, and when attention is aligned, then the exposure to failure or being eaten by a dinosaur or murdered by another tribe leader becomes an increasingly reasonable outcome. Stay in line and don't get eaten.

It is no coincidence that some of the most successful* people demonstrate some the most narcissistic tendencies. Which came first?

(*Side Note: *Success.* This is a tricky word. I can't, won't, and will not try to define the word success or successful for anyone other than myself, and even that is subject to change. For the sake of this book, let's just leave it as subjective and obscure.)

I've often said, with my own combination of arrogance and stupidity, anything is possible. This is a clear demonstration of a lack of or damage to my prefrontal cortex, or possibly because I grew up in the Portland, Oregon suburbs, where you're repeatedly told that doing your best is all that matters, while the village continues to encourage you to churn out mediocre self-portraits in just about every medium available.

Regardless, at some point, the mindset you want to have can take the wheel. And, in your comfortable delusion, not only will you stop hearing your inner voice telling you that you can't do it, but you'll start to hear the external doubters differently, too. Everyone is telling you how remarkable you are and there's no possible way things *can't* work out. Delusional? Or is it mindset? Whatever. If it gets the job done.

Doing it for the Sake of Doing it

This is the second point to look at, when considering the entrepreneur. Later in the book, we'll discuss motivation further, but this is a glance into why the word entrepreneur is even in your vocabulary and why you're reading or listening to this book in the first place. As discussed in the mindset factor, you're likely very arrogant or on your road to being a full-blown narcissist, but maybe you didn't start out that way.

So then, why are you interested in books like this in the first place? What's your project? And what are you hoping to get out of it? To be honest, it doesn't matter. And to assist with the endurance mindset, I would suggest forgetting about the end game. Just begin working on the steps to get to the next steps.

This is different than the "Why" from Simon Sinek's Golden Circle, which is absolutely critical to the success of your project, however you define it. What I hope to emphasize is this: *the next step is the most important step you are going to take, so just keep doing stuff for the sake of doing it, not for the big payout.*

Besides, sheer determination trumps talent any day of the week. Just keep going. Think about all of those Disney-type sports movies about the underdogs. Those incredible, based-on-a-true-story tales are born out of a refusal to quit mindset. When you're hearing *NO* for the 150th time, just think about who is going to play you in your underdog flick. And the road to *wherever* you want to go is even better, thanks to a character developed and molded by adversity.

Do you think we would've been able to all enjoy the classic film, *Cool Runnings*, had it not been for the will of a few determined Jamaican sprinters who, together, decided to chase Olympic dreams in a bobsled, with Jon Candy for a coach? Or what about the British kid, Eddie the Eagle, making his Olympic dreams a reality by teaching himself ski jumping against all odds, with Hugh Jackman as a coach? No. We wouldn't have amazing movies to watch, if it wasn't for the underdogs.

Last one: what about the kid from the movie *Goonies,* Sean Astin playing Rudy in the movie *Rudy,* about the kid who was determined to be a walk-on football player at Notre Dame? What about him? Astin's acting was just okay in *Goonies*, but he wasn't about to accept "just okay." He was determined to play the character Rudy.

I've never heard my brother say he doesn't know how to do something, and there is a shit-ton of stuff he doesn't know how to do. It's not so much that he thinks he is capable of doing anything and everything, but rather his not really caring whether he is able to or is allowed to. He runs on Coca Cola and not giving a fuck.

He's very successful as a business person and as a father. He's regarded as *hair on fire* in our family. Once he told us he would get a fucking horse if one more person told him not to do it, and we didn't try to call his bluff. It doesn't matter to him. It's almost like he was hit in the head at some point as a child and the part of his brain that would usually ask, "*Is this okay to be doing right now?*" just doesn't engage. There are people who will tell you to ask for forgiveness rather than permission (that's an old one), but when you act without even thinking who to ask, *that*'s when things start to just get done.

I'm a person who is generally regarded as doing whatever I want, but, in comparison to my big brother, I am a rule-follower. I am incredibly lucky to have had the influence of my renegade brother and his not-too-worried-about-what-anyone-else-thinks attitude has made a tremendous impact on my own assuredness in the business world. I can still picture the look on his face when a waiter informed him he had ordered two starches as sides to his entrée. I am pretty sure his response was, "*SO?*"

*Hey man, if you read this, thank you. And don't get a horse.

###

CHAPTER 4

YOU MAKE YOUR OWN LUCK?

The Importance of Networking

NOT EVERYONE OUT THERE is trying to stop you from achieving. So far, we have mostly looked at the opposing factors involved when pursuing goals associated with crazy ideas. But I would now like to take this time to introduce the optimist (the narcissist's friend).

There are countless people out there who want you to succeed, and they're all willing you to do so. (Probably not as many as there are wanting you to fail, and I'm an optimist, but shit, for this chapter, let's just try to be positive.) Truly: there are way more people out there than just your mom and your aunt who hope to see you crushing it.

BUSINESS BOOKS AREN'T FUNNY

These other people are not just family and friends, either. They are people who have accomplished plenty and, more than likely, have been in your shoes more than once. They are experienced and willing to give—that's right! *give*—you information and help you make connections, just to help you along the way. One day, you will do the same.

Don't just keep an eye out for these folks. Seek them out, and stay grateful for their wisdom and guidance. (Contradictory side note: lately, people have been asking me for advice in business, and even though I wrote a book on it, I still feel it is reckless to take advice from me...)

Starting a new business is going to be rough, as I'm sure you have already gathered from the beginning of this book, but it is as vital as it is brutal that we continue working *without* a massive chip on your shoulder. No one cares to work with assholes. At times, you will be totally fried and not feel like talking, texting, or emailing anyone. But there are always a few people on the journey who are down to help you.

Most successful people will tell you they had a mentor-like figure on their ride with them. There are a ton of excellent people out there with tons of information, experience, and connections, who are ready and willing to help someone with a goal, but only if you're dedicated. These outstanding people in the business world are generally eager to help the ambitious newcomers, because they had help themselves, in some form or another, and it can be especially satisfying to assist someone else. Remember: we're all some form of narcissist. The humbling act of asking for someone's help is not only healthy but can be extremely useful in terms of strategy and accomplishment.

My bread and butter has always been acting kinda stupid. Not a terrible stretch of the imagination for those who know me, but allow me to explain. I hate clichés and use them all the time—in this case, flies with honey. You know that one. I have always gotten away with murder by simply asking, "How does that work?" and then acting super-interested in whatever the answer is while remaining genuinely appreciative for the information and time spent providing it. Also, I will always be sure to ask a follow-up question, along with a compliment.

To take it too far, you might even relate it to Chuck Palahniuk's book, *Choke*, where the main character consistently goes to various restaurants and purposely causes himself to choke midway through his meal, luring a Good Samaritan into saving his life. He keeps a detailed list of everyone who saves him and sends them frequent letters about fictional bills he is unable to pay. The people feel so sorry for him, they send him cards and letters asking him about how he's doing and even continue to send him money to help him with the bills.

I am super-fortunate to have gotten major guidance and assistance from some of the folks I have worked with. You definitely don't have to be a con man to develop a quality and qualified network of mentors. Think of it as having a "guy" for that. Whether it be finding a location, securing capital, or reworking flawed electrical drawings, when you have a "guy" for that, you are in much better shape. One of the best things about curating a well-developed network of outstanding people is they likely have a pretty robust network of outstanding people they are willing to extend to you, as well.

I was working at night, making pizzas at Black Sky Brewery for Harry, one of the most talented brewers I have ever met. He's like an awesome, heavy-metal Santa Claus. I was developing my skills/educating myself, while building a network. I cut out to go see a commercial space for lease for the in-between project, when I met Jon Livaditis.

The space wasn't the right fit, but when I met Jon, we began to speak about other ventures. While we were discussing brewing, Jon asked if the reason I explained this was an in-between project was because I was really interested in brewing. He asked bluntly if I had any experience in brewing. I told him, "No, but I am working on it over at Black Sky now."

Jon's response was, "No shit! I own Black Sky."

What he meant was he owned the building but loved those tenants. He was actually hoping they would buy the building when he first came across it, but, since they were unable to (Harry and Lila are amazing, bootstrapping entrepreneurs who would never tell you they are entrepreneurs), Jon bought the building and leased it to them, so they could build their brewery.

It sounds like Jon is seriously just an amazing person who makes things happen for good people, and he is. But it took more than just calling Jon and going to look at the initial location where we first met to interest him in helping me. This is a perfect example of how sticking with it rather than accepting the word *NO* can turn into outstanding opportunities. The *NO* is figurative; Jon was down to help me find a location and get a lease signed, but the endurance required to stick with it when they're too busy to take your calls is real.

Property guys get thousands of inquiries a year from dreamers looking to kick the tires on locations when they not only don't have their shit in order, but they don't have the dedication mindset to remain persistent and see their project through till the end.

SO. What does all of this mean? It means that guys like Jon don't have time to waste, but if you stick with it and really demonstrate your eagerness to accomplish, they can help you out in tremendous ways. Real estate is generally very competitive in markets where it is worth being, and Jon set me up with a super-competitive pocket listing (a listing that isn't being advertised) in an area of the city that was ideal for my concept. Not only that, he introduced me to incredible and supportive landlords who also made the project possible and are now a very much appreciated piece of my network.

But that's just it! If you stop at the word *NO*, whether it's literally someone telling you *NO* or people just not calling you back, then it's over. Why even start in the first place?

College

I went to college and partied my way through it, going through the motions. I met some awesome people and may have even learned a thing or two. I'm a supporter of higher education for those who get it, but one of the most important lessons I did *not* receive from education was the importance of networking.

I've had extensive conversations on how networking can be done right and how it can be done very, very wrong. Every person you meet is not an opportunity to "get ahead" in life; rather, every person you meet can be an incredible opportunity to learn about what they do, why they do it, and if there's any way you can *help* them. This was kinda the missing link that divided the networking conversations: it's not about what you can get out of it, but what you can contribute, even if it's just your sincere gratitude for the chance to learn about what someone else is passionate about.

We've all met the guy who looks you up and down and asks what you do, and you can just smell it on him. The real question he is asking is, "What can you do for me?" This guy is the worst, and after I am done judging the shit out him, I start to feel sorry for him. This "what can you do for me" mentality is ultimately going to cultivate superficial and false relationships, leaving him lonely and unfulfilled.

Don't be that guy.

Too often, really great and generous people get hung up on the opposite side of wanting to be fair. Fair is great but should be looked at on a macro level, or averages. Not every transaction or interaction is going to be a direct like-for-like exchange, and the person "helping" you out isn't looking for that type of transaction, either. This overly sought desire to avoid being perceived as a "taker" is going to leave you as a "have nothing-er." (Not entirely true; kinda dramatized for effect.)

The point is yes, mutually beneficial relationships and transactions should be the goal, but they won't always go down as such, and that's okay. Okay if it helps. Consider the satisfaction of helping another person out as the reward for the advice or a favor or introduction—whatever it is that's out-benefiting you over them. And it's not to say that, down the line, your being a part of their network might not also be a huge benefit to them, when they meet someone looking to find someone who does what you do.

How about when you put your foot in your mouth because you accidentally told a total weasel about the thing you're working on? What then, smart guy?

Yep, this does happen and has happened to me. In an effort to not go on and on about a guy for whom I have zero respect and, in an attempt to not rant my frustrations, I will try to summarize the experience and what I've learned from it concisely.

NUMBER ONE: There are total fucktards out there who will steal an idea right out from under you without hesitation.

BRYAN MESSMER

NUMBER TWO: Know who you're talking to when you are building your network and marketing your concepts. If they are a little weasel, don't tell them your idea.

NUMBER THREE & FOUR: Not all competition is bad.

I was livid when the weasel not only took my idea but had the nerve to leave me with a *NO* on his way out, meaning I was told I was not capable of doing what I was setting out to do, literally. But when I was ranting to my dad about how despicable the little shit was, my dad enlightened me. "But you like competition," he reminded me.

He was right. And I hadn't thought about it this way. I do like competition. Competition breeds quality and innovation and I love America and God Bless the USA! Having caught just another *NO* from a person whom I consider subhuman wasn't the lesson. The lesson was a reminder about how much I like to win and hate to lose. His shop was definitely bad competition, because I was dealing with an unethical worm and wasn't about to trust anything he was going to do. It is unlikely he will represent the concept well in my market, and it is 100% likely he will work to steal business from me, but that's *bad* competition.

The NUMBER FOUR part of the lesson is there is such a thing as good competition, and this sounds odd. *Good competition* refers to the competitors out there who are better than you, not worse. These competitors are way more likely to be interested in collaborative efforts to elevate the concepts in a healthy manner and contribute to the momentum of the ideas.

Competitors who will challenge you to make your thing better are what you want. Plus, they're usually pretty fun to drink with. Hey, Paul and Heather, shot and a beer?

###

CHAPTER 5

"JUST BECAUSE YOU HAVE A BIG DREAM AND FOUR THOUSAND DOLLARS IN YOUR BANK ACCOUNT DOESN'T MEAN YOU DESERVE SHIT"

Raising Capital and the Word *NO*

AS YOU HAVE LIKELY gathered by now, I have a tendency to swear. I realize swearing is not the best way to convey intelligence, but I don't care. You should hear my wife speak, and she's brilliant. (Kinda late in the book for a disclaimer on language, but I bring it up now, because of the current chapter. I will try to pace myself.)

The word *NO* still sucks. Please don't stop reading because I may come off as an asshole who gets off on being denied; it sucks even more when you really need money to build something.

In this chapter, we'll explore the pain and misery of working to raise capital and the assclowns you have to deal with in order to find the money. And when I say "find the money," I should really say *"create the money,"* because it is a full-time job in itself. *BUT* do not quit your day job when you are raising capital. *Super-important to note.* Maybe the most important.

It was the devil-I-knew-type of scenario. My brother and I had secured financing, through a lending group with an SBA loan, to fund our first restaurant and repaid the loan in full in under two years. This led me to believe there was value in the relationship and it would only make sense to proceed again with this group with optimism. We obviously pursued conventional funding before the more expensive and complicated SBA option, but we took what we could get, because it was our first restaurant project of this kind and restaurants are typically high-risk for lenders.

Important note: You can pursue funding directly through the SBA; you do not need a lender.

Everything started out fine with the devil. They took my money and business plan and told me we were in good shape, shouldn't be a problem. A week passed, and I checked in on the progress: "We're working on it, looking good." Another week passed, and "Still working on it. Should have something here for you soon!" And on the third week I got, "Well, do you have any links or info on the concept? It just doesn't seem like anything anyone really knows about."

We had a problem. I said, "Well there's about forty links in the business plan I provided. Have you read the business plan?"

"I skimmed it," replied the loan officer assigned to work on my project.

"Well, maybe look at it a little closer, and let me know if you have any questions," I said with still a reasonable level of patience.

I received a phone call on the following Monday. "Bryan, it doesn't look good. There's just nothing we can do for you."

"Okay, then go ahead and refund the $900 I paid you, and I'll do this myself." I was pissed but not yet livid. Especially pissed about the time lost.

"Oh, well, uh, I don't think we can do that," he stammered.

"Why? You've skimmed my business plan, wasted my time, and now expect me to pay for that?" I asked, on my way to livid.

"It just doesn't work like that. I mean I would have to check with Mark, but I don't know."

"Tell Mark to call me."

It wasn't just about the time or money they had wasted at this point. It was falsely reassuring a relationship that was assuredly going to fail. A few days passed without my receiving a phone call—no surprise; people are typically hesitant to call others when they're pissed about a failed transaction. I called and left two messages over the next few days for Mark and let the receptionist know to expect my call the next day, as well. I'm never hostile toward receptionists ever, and I'm not really known as being a hothead, either. Here's a hint: let them politely know you're going to keep calling. If you go away, then it's over; their endurance outlasted yours.

I got my call from Mark and he was annoyed.

"What can I do for you, Bryan?" Mark started with.

"Hi Mark. Well, I'd like you to please refund my card." I was neither disrespectful nor patronizing. I seriously prefer to at least attempt a level of civility in all business.

"And why would I do that, Bryan?" Mark emphasized my name; this is a weird and offensive strategy some people use to position themselves in tense dialogue.

"Well, Mark, because your staff didn't do their jobs." Yeah, I used his first name, too, and hit the pronunciation pretty hard—I'm human.

Mark came back with, "Steve worked very hard to find you funding, but you know not everyone gets financed. That's just the way it is."

I was not livid yet, but I was starting to boil. "No, I don't think Steve did his job. And not only that, the confidence he portrayed initially was misleading. I was told several times, 'we're working on it and it looks good.'"

Mark said, "Look, just because you have $4,000 dollars in your bank account and a *big* dream doesn't mean you deserve to get financing."

And now I was livid. "So, it looks like you didn't take a real look at my accounts, either. *(I had more than $4k.)* This is exactly what I'm referring to when I say you didn't do your jobs. Go ahead and refund my card, and we'll be done here."

My heart rate had increased and I had to make a real effort not to lay into Mark for the tone he was taking and the "*big* dream" comment.

"Oh, well, I can take a look, but I don't think it's going to happen." Mark knew he was an asshole and was meekly trying to recover, because there could be money on the table.

"No, that's okay. Just refund the $900, and we'll move on." I was finished discussing anything further with Mark or anyone else at this company. Remember: you don't have to do business with anyone you don't want to. The transactions we work toward are through the network we are seeking to develop, I'd prefer not to have a jackass like Mark or his Mickey Mouse company in my network.

Mark said, "That's not how it works. You aren't guaranteed—"

"Yeah, I'm done." *Click.*

When the conversation is over, hang up the phone.

Mark followed up the conversation with an email telling me, even though I hung up on him, he was willing to refund half my money because he was the bigger man. Again, when the conversation is over, hang up. Unfortunately, you will run into Marks, but I want to believe they're still few and far between. I, of course, did not accept the partial refund, but I also didn't win the negotiation, and in some cases similar to this, you should take the money, because one dollar is better than no dollars. I had a few people in my life telling me to just accept the circumstances and take the loss, but I couldn't accept it, mostly because of how little I thought of Mark and his operation.

So, I gambled and did something I've never done: I disputed the charges. I got all of my money back.

There are a few ways to look at this. Necessity, principal, and motivation.

Necessity. It sounds crazy, but $900 was a lot of money to me. Especially when you're working toward securing more capital to make your project possible, you need every penny. It is as simple as that. You have to go through the shit, because you have to make something happen. It's not going to happen for you otherwise. And if you dig in and grit it out, then you absolutely deserve it. Bootstrapping isn't fun, but it is necessary and can be especially satisfying.

Principal. I have a tendency to do the *soapbox* thing, but I'm a fairly passionate and opinionated person when it comes to what I feel is right and wrong. Plus, fuck him. I have to get into *it* because I believe in something and can't ignore it.

Motivation. A special thank you to Mark and other assholes like him. I cannot deny the comment *"big* dream" stuck with me. I use every instance of the word *NO* to fuel my drive to continue. It's sick, but sometimes I actually enjoy getting shut down, just because it makes me work that much harder.

Raising money vs. saving money

We live and work in a time where venture capitalist is a job title. A pretty sweet job title, but I believe the VC availability and angel investor concepts can actually hinder your drive and relieve you of some satisfaction.

Obviously, it is still not easy to just convince someone to loan or give you money, but the problem with having such a prevalent venture system in our culture isn't just the potential for diluted satisfaction and equity, but people forget there is another way.

Save your money, start small, and scale up at an appropriate rate. A lot of VCs aren't very patient, either: they want a return on the investment as soon as possible, possibly creating a misplaced emphasis on the company's vision and challenging motivations. I am absolutely not saying to turn down a generous VC who is interested in supporting your goals, but it is very important to remain pragmatic when entering into an agreement, especially if there is an equity deal in the mix.

Giving up equity is always a tricky situation. Sometimes, it makes total sense, and sometimes, you're feeling so desperate to get the project to the next level, you think it is the only way this is ever going to happen. What percentage of the guests on

Shark Tank do you think hit the carpet and have to bite their tongues to keep from shouting *"DEAL!"*

You can do this without giving up equity to an investor, but it is all about how you want your company to look in five or ten years. None of this is easy. You may even have people trying to force money into your pockets because they care about you and want to help. Be careful. You take money from your brother, and the entire family dynamic is on the table.

So, if you're not supposed to do the VC-for-equity thing, you can't secure conventional financing, you're not rich, and you shouldn't take money from family, then what the fuck are we even doing here?!

Great question.

Save your money. Every penny. You will be shocked when you realize what you're capable of putting together and how far you can stretch a buck, especially if you have an idea that's worth something. The satisfaction of your accomplishments will be amplified by 1,000.

Another option, also not easy, is to seek out a microlender. Microlenders exist to facilitate loans, usually to underfunded and under-collateralized business ventures. Typically, these lenders will have an SBA-backed program that is suitable for you. Not only that, these are amazing people, very interested in being a part of your story and creating opportunities.

And the last fucked-up way we've all heard about is maxing out some credit cards. This is insane and super-dangerous but, unfortunately, necessary at times. Just whatever you do, remember: maxing out can still be intelligent and pragmatic.

Also, remember this mantra: *Every dollar you save is the same as a dollar you make.*

Good luck, you frugal sonofabitch.

###

CHAPTER 6

BEAUTIFUL DENVER, COLORADO

The City and the Fine People Who Work There: More *NO*

OKAY, AFTER THE JOURNEY with Mark in the last chapter, I'd like to take it back to something a little less miserable. But that's not going to happen. Why is that not going to happen? Because this is a chapter about getting kicked in the nuts over and over again.

But there's a lesson in here somewhere, I'm pretty sure.

There is a way around this part, kinda, but when you're bootstrapping, like so many people do, every dollar you save is the same as a dollar made. If you're able to have a trusted contractor do the work for you, then they will make the hellish journey to the city to work on securing permits for you, and they also have the experience and connections. If you're not literally building a business (specifically, a brick-and-mortar business with a storefront), then you're one of the smart ones; however, there are still nonstop challenges and all sorts of *NOs* to overcome. There is not a single business in the history of commerce that comes with profits worth having without the headaches and suffering required to get there. It's the excruciating process of getting there that makes it worth doing.

Plus, there is something to be said for learning through the experience, not just reading books written by hacks.

While reading the next example try to contemplate the last *NO* you received and anticipate the upcoming *NO* that's waiting for you around the next turn. Apply your own experiences to the method of smiling and adopting the demeanor of a Golden Retriever while someone is hammering at your will to go on, and just see what happens.

When it is time to submit drawings (architectural and MEPs), you first need to go through zoning. If you've been through this before, you're likely thinking, *Yeah, right, Bryan, you stupid jerk. There is no way your stupid "act stupid and polite" method did anything to help you here*, but wait! Don't stop reading!

I know how it sounds, and trust me, I would be thinking the same exact thing. If you haven't had the pleasure of making the trip down to your local building department yet, just imagine a group of people all named *Thad* gathered together to make your life a living hell. Because of each Thad's pain during adolescence, this is not just a career for them; it is a vocation. I wasn't a bully, Thad! I promise!

Anyway, you will need to get the zoning stamp before you can log in plans. Different municipalities obviously have different "take a number" procedures for being seen, but generally you just wait and wait and wait. If you're the first person to the zoning window, you'd think you're in great shape, but you're wrong. Even though it is a quarter past the time they were supposed to get to seeing people, they are still not ready to work: still busy going over last night's *Game of Thrones* and stirring coffee. So, you have to make the most of the opportunity.

When you make it to the window, you will immediately be told you do *NOT* have what you need, even though you do, because you're prepared. This is a trick so they can send you away and clock out for the first break of the day. So, what do you do? You plaster on the dumbest and most excited look you can and say, "Thank you!" And then you settle in. It's all about endurance. Spread out your shit on their desk or table *OR* whatever, and begin telling them how excited you are about your project and how you can't wait for it to be open. And also tell them how they will definitely have to come check it out! Think of a Golden Retriever.

They're going to continue to shut it down, because they can. You've demonstrated how excited you are and spread out your gear like a traveling window salesman would, as soon as they get into your home. Now, to add in a little extra stupid, just start asking questions and nodding like you get it. You're on the same team, and you want him to get to the next coffee break even worse than he does, but you just can't go without that stamp!

"Thank you so much for helping me. I *really* appreciate it, I didn't know that. It makes such a huge difference to have people like you helping me out with this stuff. I honestly can't imagine trying to get through this without people like you helping me. Seriously. Thank you. How do you stay on top of all of this? Especially with how things seem to be constantly changing... I couldn't do it. It's impressive."

Memorize that, if you have to.

It won't work every time.

But if you get one on the hook and remember their name and maybe even follow up with a thank-you email, then they can start to feel involved in fighting the good fight with you.

Take away: The more excited and dumb you look, the more people are likely to help you. People help me all the time.

Googling and Networking

Since there was Googling, people have been Googling each other and themselves. We're all guilty of that. But *why* are we Googling each other?

Sometimes, it's for a really creepy reason. Other times, it's for really creepy reasons. In business, however, it can be exceptionally useful to gather a little more information about a person.

I will absolutely research the people I am trying to work with, mainly in hopes of finding some common ground we may be able to connect on. I am not saying this is the first thing I do. Rather, it's a way to hopefully find a connection when there hasn't been time to do so in the first interaction and there likely will not be enough time going forward. Like I said, creepy.

Okay, to put this into some context, I'll take you back to the City of Denver Building Department and the plan reviewers.

Not all of the plan reviewers were total bummers, but one very critical reviewer held my fate in his hands and was ready to torture me into bankruptcy for no other reason than that's how he gets off (I'm assuming).

I again tried to make every effort to be open and appreciative and as ass-kissing as possible, in order to hopefully move the project forward, but after weeks (not exaggerating) of time/money lost, I still couldn't make this thing move.

I Googled the guy.

I found out who his rabbi was and then promptly went to the synagogue and converted to Judaism. It wasn't that big of a deal for me; I formerly aligned with the Christian atheists. But now I'm a Jew.

Okay, that's not exactly how this went, but I was able to find out that he was active in the Jewish community and had previously owned his own architecture firm. The Jewish part didn't really help me (I enjoy Easter candy too much to convert), but the former business owner piece gave me something to empathize and commiserate over. And that's exactly what I did. I didn't blatantly come out and ask him why he's not in business for himself any longer, but I did take a subtle tone in future emails about how underappreciated the rules are and how the code is the code and shouldn't be interpreted as much as it should be applied. Then I signed off:

Gotta go shopping for T-square.

Your friend,

Bryan.

More or less.

The empathetic route, combined with the overly exaggerated appreciation for what was important **to him**, moved the project forward and literally saved me tens of thousands of dollars. But then I got caught.

I was back at the City Building (I think disputing a parking ticket—money saved = money earned), when I saw the architectural plan reviewer in the foyer. I thought this would be a good opportunity to introduce myself in person and thank him for all his *help* in getting my project completed plus remind him how integral he had been in our shared success. The thought is always to reinforce your network to hopefully alleviate some of the pain on your next project.

I went across the lobby where he was enjoying some free snacks provided by the group occupying the common space that day to promote something or other. I said hello and introduced myself and then went into the whole appreciation spiel. Things were going pretty smoothly, and I was unnecessarily proud of my decision to build that network.

He seemed pretty good, even flattered, and then he asked, "One more question—how did you know who I was?"

I didn't realize I had no way of explaining how I would've been able to pick the little paranoid sonofabitch out of a crowd that didn't make me look like a stalker. Remember, I Googled him; there was no employee of the month photo of him on the wall behind him...

"Oh!" I stammered. "I research everyone I'm working with. Not in weird way. I'm not going to come to your house or anything. Okay, well, good meeting you. Thanks for everything. Bye." That's pretty much verbatim.

So maybe the takeaway is to stop patting yourself on the back and pull your head out before a city plan reviewer gets a restraining order against you? No. Let's stick with the "Googling people is creepy" but still can provide some potential leverage to utilize when working with others to accomplish a shared goal.

###

CHAPTER 7

READ THE RIGHT BOOKS

Borrowed/Stolen Ideas That Inspire Me

THIS IS A GOOD OPPORTUNITY for caution. Caution: Do not overeducate yourself to the point of immobility.

Believe me, this happens. Too often, the ambitious will stunt their progress by falling into a "research and educate" loop. It is absolutely imperative to know about what you are trying to do, inside and out, but you can only really know what it's about by getting your hands dirty. If you continue to proceed with the research phase to an unwarranted extent, you are never going to actually take the leap. You'll continue to tell yourself you're not ready yet, just need a little more time to research, gotta make sure everything has been figured out to the nth degree, but really, you're just procrastinating out of fear, and you'll likely end up doing nothing at all, or, worse, you'll open a froyo franchise.

Now that the caution is out of the way, I can confirm: books *can* provide motivation and lessons.

Start with Why by Simon Sinek:

Start with Why is something everyone should read before they get started and again once their business has been operating for a few months. Simon breaks it down with the Golden Circle, and, if consistently applied to the operations of your business, your chances of success improve drastically.

"*WHY* is the filter for decision making."

Shoe Dog by Phil Knight:

Phil Knight started Nike when he was in his late twenties. Obviously, not every venture will turn into a billion-dollar movement, but *Shoe Dog* is an amazingly recounted journey of struggles that anyone working to build a business can relate to. It makes a massive difference, knowing you're not alone, when the world around you is trying to stop you from getting to the next step. Phil's journey to build Nike and the many lessons in humility that came with it can make any entrepreneur feel like there's hope.

Anything You Want by Derek Sivers:

This book can be read in an hour and can again put gas in the tank to help you keep going. Derek created CD Baby and really built something out of nothing by accident. His insights are especially refreshing, considering his lack of a formal business background.

"Building a company is like creating your own utopia."

Let My People Go Surfing by Yvon Chouinard:

"The education of a reluctant business man" is the subtitle of the founder of Patagonia's book. It really sums it up: it is the case of another awesome person doing something for the sake of doing it, and if anyone has a *WHY* that they stick to, it's Yvon Chouinard. Patagonia is an amazing example of dedication to core values. I especially appreciate this story for the sake of rejecting what others tell you to do and expect you to do.

"Identify the goal, and then forget about it and focus on the process."

A Guide to the Good Life: The Ancient Art of Stoic Joy by William B. Irvine:

This one isn't a business-focused story, but it is definitely worth reading while you're thinking about and developing your *WHY*. Irvine describes Stoic philosophy, one of the most popular and successful schools of thought in ancient Rome, and shows how its insights can be adapted and applied to our daily lives.

"Thinking is an object of wisdom."

There are tons of books worth having a hardcopy of, to look back on and fuel your fire when you're running out of energy and need motivation to continue. And I don't know who said it, but "leaders are readers," and that is absolutely true. Not just for the motivation aspect should you be reading these amazing people's work, but also for the opportunity to learn from what they did right and what they did wrong.

You're writing your book as we speak.

You can also do a lot of the right listening. I'm not a big podcast person, simply because I tend to zone out, but the *How I Built This* podcast with Guy Raz is an incredible resource for inspiration and information. Guy interviews all types of entrepreneurs and gets authentic takes on their experiences and what it was like to build their companies, and how they feel about it, now and then.

The live interview with Howard Schultz, two-time CEO of Starbucks, will shed incredible light on the crazy beginnings that company had and the tumultuous period the company survived. The podcast is much like the biographies and books written on and about the entrepreneurial experience.

The reason the podcast can be especially useful, other than the super-successful people sharing their wisdom, is how the light of the shared struggle shows through in every interview. There aren't many interesting stories about how a successful head of a company was just handed everything. It is always a chewed-up and painful road to success. It makes a massive difference to hear about it from the people who have been there and made it.

###

CHAPTER 8

GOOD PEOPLE CAN STILL GIVE BAD ADVICE

Self-leveling Concrete and the Assholes at Home Depot: A Different Type of *NO*

AS I MENTIONED previously, bootstrapping isn't really a choice for most people. I don't think there has ever been someone out there who began a project thinking, *You know, I really would prefer to have less money to make this dream a reality.*

But nonetheless, bootstrapping can be a tremendous vehicle for learning things the hard way. And when you learn things the hard way, you generally don't forget the lesson anytime soon.

You're going to have to get your hands dirty again and again. Whether you're pouring concrete or fucking with SEO and web stuff, it doesn't matter: people are going to attempt to help you. Please notice I use the word *attempt* here. Remember from the last chapter, when we learned how it's good to look dumb and excited? Well, this is going to attract kind-hearted idiots sometimes.

I was at a dog park not too long ago, and this jabroni was telling some chick all about how he had trained his German Shepherd to respond to German commands. *AND* then, you know what he did? He threw a frisbee golf disc way up into the air, and it came shooting down into the face a woman reading a book quietly by herself. Then the German Shepherd jumped all over the woman who had just been struck in the face with a heavy-ass frisbee outta nowhere, and the guy just started yelling, *"Nein! Nein!"* Like the fucking dog actually *knew* German!

The dog did not know German. What we're getting at here is that stupid people exist and they're gonna want to help, too.

On that note, you may hear this phrase way more often than you'd like, while working to complete your goals: "Well, at least you're learning a lot." It is rough hearing this over and over again, even though it is true and the people saying it really have the best intention. But shit, is it brutal! You probably didn't set out to learn anything. Rather, you're trying to create something against all odds.

Good people can give horrible advice! It is a serious challenge to separate the actual experts from the people who are nice and want to be helpful but have no fucking clue what they are talking about.. Try to forgive them when they cost you time and money and heartache: they didn't mean it.

Here's a tip! The people who work at Home Depot are not helpful! I don't want to berate the fine people at the Depot, because I'm sure many of them are lovely people. However, they are totally fucking worthless when it comes to any type of direction or expertise. *DO NOT ASK* them for help. Depending on the department they work in, they have either failed at their profession or just saw a sign that said the Depot was hiring and thought, *What the hell?*

You must be thinking, *Wow, Bryan must have really gotten burned by the fine folks at Home Depot. I like Home Depot. I do the birdhouse-building classes on the weekend, and they're enthralling!* If you actually do build the birdhouses or whatever at the Depot on the weekends, then stop reading here and do not try to open your own business. It's just not for you.

Yes, I made the mistake a number of times of trusting the people in the orange aprons. And they seemed so wise and crusty…, it was too tempting. (Actually, the dude who hooked me up with self-leveling concrete to build four shower pans was actually a younger guy with a beard, so I guess don't trust people with beards?)

I know how that sounds—not the people-with-beards part, but the fact that I'm the dumbass who mixed up self-leveling concrete to build shower pans. But I really *did* throw up my hands, explain that I had never worked with concrete before, and showed him a picture of exactly what it was I was doing and what needed to be done. I even asked, "Are you sure this is the stuff I need? And is this the most forgiving, for a rookie like me?"

Well, as implied in the name, I built beautiful and perfectly level shower pans! When the plumbing inspector came to take a look at what I had done, he was so impressed at how level I had made the shower floors, he was like, "Did you slope these?" Even better, it was Christmas Eve when I'd scheduled this particular inspection, and I was hoping he would give me a pass, in the holiday spirit. And he probably would have, but the shower floors were so perfectly level that, when he turned on the water, it went everywhere except down the drain.

Does this seem like a big deal to you? Here's the thing: not only is it especially excruciating to waste money when you're bootstrapping, but the time lost is intensely concerning. Typically, when you negotiate a commercial lease agreement, you have what is called "free rent." It is a period of time allotted to building out the space for your business, and landlords do not collect rent for a period of time because you aren't yet open for business and generating any revenue. Time is literally money. The bearded fuck at Home Depot didn't realize the implications of his stupid, horrible guidance. He's not malicious under that beard. This is exactly the lesson learned, though: good people can give absolute horseshit advice, so be very careful as you proceed and manage the risks to the best of your ability.

Now, not every person is going to have to get their hands dirty to this extent. Self-leveling concrete is not likely a scenario that sneaks up and bites *you* in the ass. But it's a metaphor. Okay, it's not exactly a metaphor, but you can imagine there are enough circumstances where you have to be especially mindful of making mistakes or you won't even realize you have made a mistake until it shows up later.

For instance, the critical importance of having an optimized website. Most businesses will rely on a website to drive traffic, regardless of the industry you're in. The complexities of optimizing a website are much greater than I think most people give credit. It seems so simple to Google something and find it, right? But there are an incredible number of businesses that flounder or fail because they are buried on the next pages of the search engine.

So, what do you do? You're going to have to hire a professional. You cannot just slam together a website on a free platform and do a little Facebooking and expect people to find you. And it's not that simple. But hiring a solid SEO firm isn't simple, either. It is crazy how many of those firms are out there, and they will all tell you the same thing: they'll make you famous. How do you measure the return on your investment with so many variables impacting your presence online?

SEO firms and the concept of search engine optimization is a great example of how complicated things can get for a couple of reasons. You can find an SEO company on the web, or you can have a friend refer one they have used previously. If you find a company online, you would think it's a safe bet, because clearly, they have a strong web presence since you found them. But you need to keep in mind the resources available to larger companies. Do not make the assumption you will have the same *means* or that they will be interested in dedicating the time and energy required to make *your* online presence exceptional. They will take a retainer and tell you how many hours they're going to have to spend; they will build a tremendous amount of value into their pitch. But you still don't know whether it's worth it.

So, you ask a friend and hope they have some positive results from a company they've worked with, but again, here is the potential for good people to provide bad advice. I'm guilty of this, too. I have told people—people I care about, unsolicited—that, "Oh yeah, these guys are great," before I've even really found out what type of impact the experience is going to have. I didn't do it on purpose; I was just trying to help. Once, we even referred the absolute worst contractor on the planet to an unsuspecting couple when we were only a month into our project. You think you know someone, right?!

Here's the deal: vet the companies and people you're working with, and know whether you're going to get the quality of goods and services you require. Even this book— don't just take anything you read for fact; take it at face value, and find out for yourself what works and what doesn't.

Just because the chicken has a green label doesn't make it organic. And just because they're wearing an orange apron and a beard doesn't mean they're qualified to advise you on anything.

Mine is the experience of a rookie contractor (also seen in the "You don't know what you don't know" chapter). You'd think, by hiring subcontractors, you've covered the skilled-labor pieces of the job and you're clear to go across the street for burgers and beers with the visiting in-laws, right?

Wrong. If you have a solid contractor in your network, send him a Christmas card at the very least; they have insanely difficult jobs. Every professional working your project still must be supervised. And speak up! Not asking questions out of concern of being exposed will come back to bite you. Ask them, and then ask yourself if that's the way you want to see it done. I have had the privilege of working with some really excellent subs, but I have also worked with too many who just wanted to get the job done the quickest and easiest way possible.

And another thing: the good guys might be thinking they are doing everything the way you want it done, but they don't know exactly what you're thinking. Do not tell any of them just to do what is normally done and think it will be all fine. You're going to have to get your hands dirty and stay attentive. As soon as you run out of energy, things will go to shit. Be specific about how things should look and function when completed. Lead them and you'll be much happier with the results.

Note on Balance: Running out of energy is inevitable. Without an outlet to shut down and recharge, you're not going to last long doing the hundred-hour weeks marathon. Find something that allows you to unplug/detach, and then force yourself to do it. This is something different from finding the balance in your personal relationship.

###

CHAPTER 9

MOVING A MOUNTAIN ONE SLAB OF CONCRETE AT A TIME

The Pyramids were Built by Drunks

"Anyone who quotes Confucius is a dick."

–Anonymous

IT'S HARD TO RELAX when you've just crushed your hand between a concrete wall and a 2' x 2' x 6" slab of concrete (the weight of concrete is approximately 150 pounds per cubic foot). For exaggeration's sake, I'll say it weighed 289 pounds!

But wait. Why were you stacking concrete slabs in the first place? That doesn't seem business-like at all, does it? Who did you vote for?

Right. I understand this is sounding weird, so allow me to explain the bootstrapping thing again. I needed to save money wherever possible, so, when the concrete guys cut nearly 400 linear feet of concrete out of the basement where I was building the first Easy Float, I told them not to worry about removing the concrete blocks. They wanted $3,000 to take the cut slabs of concrete out the basement, and I said, "Does it say sucker on my forehead?! I don't think so!"

So, I decided I would pull every stone from out of the trench and stack them neatly under the stairs, since the building department told me I would have to wall off the cavern under the stairs anyway. The dudes cutting the concrete looked at me with pity: they were nice people, and I think they threw in a few linear feet on the house.

I figured I'd get started, eager to get my hands dirty and get the show on the road. Time lost in plan review was already killin' me on the free rent. I took my shovel and pried the first block from the trench, flipped it over, and then tilted it up on to a hand truck. I wheeled it over to the tomb I was creating and jammed it as far back as I could get it. Not so bad, I thought. Just about one hundred more to go.

By slab eighteen, I was toast. It was absolutely brutal, and I was having to begin stacking the slabs up onto each other by rolling them end over end, to ensure there would be enough space under the stairs to fit all of them under there. My back was killing me, my shoulder was jacked (not in a good way), and I thought there was no way I was going to finish this in one night. But I decided I would get as much done as I possibly could and feel good about myself for saving money, bootstrapping this sonofabitch. (Notice I am working at night in this story. Because working day and night is better than working for someone else.)

I was approaching the halfway point, and the stack under the stairs was getting larger, when I received a text from my point person for the plumbing subs (subcontractors). He was letting me know the crew to dig the trenches for the drains would be there in the morning. And if you've ever been through building anything brick-and-mortar, whether you have a contractor or you did it yourself, you know you do *not* want to try to reschedule a sub and potentially delay the next steps and inspections ever.

At this time in the Denver area, the good subs were few and far between, and some inspectors could be booked out weeks. It was a boomtown in 2016, and you definitely did not want to be the cause of delays on your own project.

I texted him back, "*Cool*," and told myself to stop being a punk and get back to work. This is when I lost control of a slab at the top of the stack. It rolled sideways and crushed the middle knuckle on my right hand between the wall and the slab. I was sure it was broken. Imagine a 300-pound block of concrete smashing your hand against more concrete.

"*FUCK*!" That's what I yelled. And I wish I had a picture to include at this point in the book. My hand was gross but not broken.

I paused the Lou Reed in my headphones and called my wife.

"Hey, how's everything going down there?" she asked.

"Pretty good. Just slammed my hand between the concrete and the wall. Not good," I told her.

"Oh no! Honey, is it broken?" She pronounces *honey* different in these cases, more like *HUN-knee*.

I said, "No, just *feels* broken."

"Well, you better call it a night and come home."

"I can't. I'm not finished, and the plumbers are going to be here in the morning."

"Okay. I'll bring you some spaghetti and beer. Need anything else?" she asked seriously.

"That'd be great. Thank you."

You probably think my wife and I are hillbillies who treat potentially broken bones with pasta and beer, and I guess you're kinda right!

Actually, Emily is a very talented Family Nurse Practitioner, and one thing about NPs: they are possibly the most holistic crowd in Western medicine. The first step is effectively treating your patient is to know your patient, and Emily knows me well.

I scarfed the spaghetti, and while I guzzled beer from the growler Em had brought, I thought about the pyramids. Granted, the pyramids were built on slave labor, which is never cool, but the workforce was also sustained on a fermented soup-type beer that provided the necessary sustenance to go on and build a modern marvel.

Back to the point. When you're struggling to continue, there is an opportunity. This reflection is not intended to reemphasize the importance of bootstrapping or to write *on and on* about how cool Emily is, but rather to highlight the importance of endurance.

I was going to title this book, *Kicked in the Nuts One Hundred Times*, because of instances like getting my hand crushed when the plumbers were coming the next day. It's a choice to suck it up and deal with the adversities coming your way. It won't always be another organization jacking you up on the journey. Sometimes, it's just gravity.

Takeaways*?*

- ✓ What are you going to do when you get a hand smashed?

###

CHAPTER 10

WHO YOU ARE ACCOUNTABLE TO WILL MAKE A BIG DIFFERENCE

When You Feel like Stopping

THIS IS A BASIC SUGGESTION to kick off this chapter, and it can be kind of like a precaution, I guess. But, like every relationship, business relationships are also very unique from one to the next. SO. When it comes time to pursue whatever it is you're interested in doing, whether it is your first business or your tenth, keep in mind the relationship with whatever partner you might choose to work with will be tested.

It definitely seems like an awesome idea to work with a friend on a shared passion and turn that passion into a vocation in which you both make money and revel in the satisfaction of accomplishment. But, like most things, this is easier said than done.

Family-owned businesses. They're f-ing miserable, thanks to a preexisting dynamic that has been in place since they were in diapers. I'm sure there are businesses operated by families or family members that are flourishing, but the odds are not good.

Please do not learn this lesson the hard way. There are too many friendships lost, happy families turned bitter, and relationships that have gone cold because it seemed like a good idea. There is a very simple way to avoid having a precious relationship turned to collateral damage on the rise to success or, realistically, the downward spiral of failure and misery (when things go wrong because you didn't heed the warning): Get your ducks in a row *LEGALLY*.

When your best bud wants to create the CBD company to end all CBD companies, put down the beers for a minute, and get your shit together. It will make all the difference in the end, when there is something to fall back on and refer to, if your assumptions turn out to be fucked. And it will be so, *so* good for the relationship to be able to ditch the accountability of being like, "I don't think so, dude. That's not how we set this thing up." Instead of, "F-you, Karl. You can eat shit. I'm not responsible for that, and I want out. And you're fired!"

*I cannot stress this enough: Get the shit lined up and agreed on before proceeding. You don't even have to know exactly what it is you're lining up right at this very moment! That's what lawyers are for. Lawyers are expensive, but nowhere near as expensive as lawsuits.

If you can do it without a partner, that's generally recommended, for several reasons. But there are also tons of pros to sharing the experience with someone. All that said, it can also be exceptionally useful to have someone or a group/team to share the responsibility and work load with, too. And eventually you'll have incredible people, if you lead and keep leading.

This brings me to the point of the title of this chapter , "Who You are Accountable to will Make a Big Difference... When You Feel like Stopping." It can be too easy to quit when you only have yourself to be accountable to.

When I began working toward building Easy Float, the business that inspired this book, I originally had a partner on the ride with me. We were fifty-fifty, and he is actually a great friend from college who originally told me about the concept. We didn't do any of the things mentioned previously with regards to defining the division of labor or what would happen in the case of a buyout, or really anything that would have been useful in saving our friendship, had something gone terribly wrong. It's called an Operating Agreement. However, my partner got cold feet about moving to Colorado and setting up shop, a few months into the "securing a location" part of our planning phases.

It wasn't anything more than he didn't think he wanted to make the move, and that was totally okay. These things happen, and it definitely threw a wrench into the project and my ability to complete it with the means and resources I was left with. But having him on board initially did something pretty excellent, and I'm not sure I wouldn't have quit, were it not for having to be accountable to someone else.

It sounds kinda weird, right? Even more so, writing it or saying it out loud. But that's the truth, and a pretty massive shot in the "pro" column, having another person to be accountable to.

I'm a big fan of Tim Ferris's interview with the guy who invented http:/ (Hypertext Transfer Protocol), Marc Andreessen. He refused to answer the question, "What would you have done different?" because it is a useless exercise. We cannot go back, so he only looks forward.

And while you're looking forward and doing everything you can to plan and anticipate and apply what you've learned from the mistakes of others, it helps to have another person in the mix to have to consider, especially when things get rough or you get distracted by another interesting project you'd like to pursue. We are a society of ADD: even the adults have it.

If you don't have anyone keeping you on the hook to see the project through to completion, then just start telling everyone about what you're doing. Keep yourself accountable to keep it going, even though a lot of *entrepreneurial types* generally don't give a shit about what others think. Try it out anyway, and treat it like an exercise in having people laugh at your crazy idea.

Past the point of no return: that's where you have to get before the other person you're accountable to bails. It generally comes quickly, but you can apply perspective to decide when that point arrives. For instance, if you've put in the time researching and preparing but haven't even put a single dollar into the project, the time invested *can* be enough to not turn back. As soon as you secure the capital and money is in the business account, or when you ink up your lease, these "no turning back moments" are unmistakable.

No turning back is an excellent and scary place to be, but it can definitely be super-overwhelming, too. You'll read all about the people who hung in there, and they will describe the no-turning-back anxiety as a key motivator in making it happen no matter the odds.

Takeaways*:*

- ✓ When you tell people you're going to do something, you're on the hook to do it, and that's a good thing.
- ✓ Tell everyone.
- ✓ When your back is against the wall, you're going to figure it out.

###

CHAPTER 11

BLUE RIBBON IN 1970-SOMETHING

Phil Did It and So Did Other Humans

IT'S HARD TO IMAGINE Nike being anything other than the powerhouse it is today. But everyone has to start somewhere. I've read *Shoe Dog* several times, but when I read it for the first time, it made an enormous difference by refilling my tank in the middle of the project from hell that inspired this book. The stories from *Shoe Dog,* and other books like it, made it possible for me to keep going when I didn't think I had anything left.

I borrowed the book from a friend who recommended I keep it, and I honestly didn't think I had the time to get through a full book (not just listen to it or speed read, but really read). I was busy wearing the different hats of a solo entrepreneur, working tirelessly to learn what I didn't know, and striving for any forward progress I could possibly achieve. I didn't think I had time or could afford to share any of my focus with anything but the project, especially not a book.

When I picked up *Shoe Dog,* I couldn't put it down. I finished it in three days and the timing couldn't have been better.

So, thanks for the book review, dipshit. What's the point?

(I would've thought the same thing had I not been the one writing....)

The point is the struggle of the billionaire shoe mogul isn't an easy one to relate to when you're barely scraping by or crossing your fingers on a phone call with a lender or just feeling like there's no end in sight. When Phil Knight shares a story about how he had to pull the name of his company out of his ass in a boardroom filled with Japanese shoe manufacturers, I thought, *Okay, I'm not alone.* When he states plainly he just wants to know if it's going to work or is it over, I've desired the same answers.

At the point when Nike was unable to borrow money, even with the bank they had been dedicated to for years, it seemed hopeless. Been there.

Takeaway:

✓ I don't care if I ever earn billions: I don't plan to, and I'm not working to. And I definitely don't expect to. But neither did Phil.

###

CHAPTER 12

YOU DON'T KNOW WHAT YOU DON'T KNOW

Mistakes Are Sometimes Unavoidable

SOUNDS PAINFULLY OBVIOUS. You're thinking, *I knew this book was dog shit written by a hack, but come on...* Yeah, I would think the same thing, and I'm not saying you're that far off. But just consider the statement for a few moments, and then think again or skip the chapter—it doesn't matter to me.

The *you don't know what you don't know* can cost you tens of thousands of dollars, your business's reputation, your entire business, or all of the above. Even worse, it can severely damage your network, if you don't handle the adversity properly and effectively. Once in a while, you're going to fuck it up pretty bad, but it won't always be your fault, and that can make it sting slightly less. These unforeseen fuckups are one reason why it is so critical to manage and attempt to mitigate as much risk as you can possibly anticipate. This gives you a "fuck it up" cushion of sorts.

Most folks reading books like this one are also Do-It-Yourself types and generally comfortable with risk, but you cannot do everything. Hiring an architect, engineer, electrician, or the like is inevitable and crucial. Trying to do your own electrical is not only impractical, but probably illegal and definitely dangerous. You're taking a risk, hiring certain trades and professions, whether they're building/optimizing your website or getting your engineered drawings. But you're going to have to trust that some people know what they're doing and can be trusted to do it right. You have too many other aspects to manage. There's no time to learn the engineering of the MEPs or even how to read drawings like a professional.

Most of the time, your network won't refer you to a hack, but that shit does happen. This is another example of bad advice from good people, though not quite as easy to discern, because these people aren't usually wearing orange aprons. My own float project was victim of the absolute worst engineer you can find. A type of *NO* mixed with another kick in the nuts, in the end. With the amount of building that was going on at the time in Denver, pickings were slim. Kind of a once-removed cousin to someone in my network I relied on. (Update: the referrer is out of the network.)

I paid top dollar for those plans. Up front. I crammed them through the building department's plan review process, received legitimate bids on these plans, and was prepared to build the entire project off of these beautiful plans until the electrician took a look at them in the real world and said, "These plans are shit."

"But I paid *top* dollar for these plans. These are good plans!" I pleaded with the electrician, who had done previous projects and is a very trustworthy and competent person. I, on the other hand, didn't know how to even read electrical drawings.

They were indeed shit. We decided to scour the building to confirm there wasn't something missed, like an additional electrical service or panel hiding somewhere. But Neil the electrician was right: the plans were shit.

We called the engineer to ask what we could do, and his response was, "Well, what else could this thing be?" He was serious. This was his solution to his lazy, shit work.

WHAT else could the business be?! Oh, I don't know—maybe I'll just drop all the research and planning from my current business planning and sell fucking mittens!

In the end, I became great friends with Neil the electrician, and we bonded over yelling, "*KIRKMAN!*" (the engineer) for the rest of the project when anything would go wrong. I am very grateful to have dudes like Neil in my network.

As far as not knowing what you don't know, I had no idea what to look for on professionally drawn and stamped electrical drawings. I had to ask my developer landlords a few times if *this* was my fault for being a rookie, and they reassured me each time that this shit happens and that's why you hire a stamp-carrying professional to get shit done right. You're not an engineer. You're not supposed to know this shit.

As nice as it is to hear from experienced people you respect that you didn't fuck up and are not the direct cause of the delay, it is still a situation that will need to be handled, and it's up to you to recover to the best of your ability and just keep going. Maybe give Larry a call and let him have it.

Just bad luck. Just keep going.

###

CHAPTER 13

IT'S LIKE THE TIME THEY KILLED MY BROTHER

You Can't Even Remember the Last Massive Problem Because...

AS YOU CAN PROBABLY imagine, the electrical problem caused by some Mickey Mouse electrical drawings wasn't resolved overnight. The plans had to be entirely redrawn, re-permitted, almost repaid for (*almost*), and then the power company had to be involved, in order to deliver a new power service and meter to a building that was nearly maxed out. We built this entire business on one extension cord, in the meantime.

I tried to remain positive and make the connections I could and needed with the power company, while still trying to push the project forward and avoid any further delays. *I would like to run on with exactly what happened, but this part of the story is a book in itself, so check out the endnotes, if you're interested in what occurred with the electrical company. Or better, email me directly… There are no endnotes.

I was ready to turn on the lights after two months of working in the dark, an eager beaver, when the power company arrived for the second time. (The first time, I hadn't passed the inspection, even though I said I had.) Well, the inspector, who is actually a pretty cool guy, demanded we switch around some pretty hefty wires and change some shit from the way the power company had arranged everything, before we could pass. Neil and I both thought it was probably a better idea to listen to our forty-plus-year lineman, instead, since he was the one who worked in the field day in and day out, but we changed it up anyway, because that's what you do when you're trying to pass an inspection. You do what the inspector tells you to do.

With the hefty wires switched around and the inspection passed, I called the lineman back out to the job to flip the switch. And to be clear, the lineman is the guy who works for the power company: old school guy. He doesn't switch around hefty wires he already installed just because you want to pass an inspection.

"Ready to light this candle?" Mark the lineman asked. He's an excellent dude.

"You bet, Mark. Can't wait to see how much shit I need to fix," I joked to him. "Quick question, though. The inspector had us reverse these two fat wires going into the panel. Is that going to be a problem?"

"Shit yes, that's a problem, Bryan. Shit.' Mark was serious. "All of your damn lights would've have blown up, if we'd turn this thing on the way it is."

"*Fuck*!" I was serious, too. "Shit goddamit. I cannot believe this shit. Sorry—you know I'm not pissed at you. Thank you. I really appreciate it." I reiterated how appreciative I was for Mark having his head on straight.

"Yeah, Bryan, just 'cuz you remove the tape from one line and put it on the other, it doesn't change the voltage." Mark wasn't being an asshole; to clarify, he was equally pissed off at the inspector. "I've been a lineman for more than forty years, and it has always been red on the right. *Always*. And we're not going to change that."

"Okay, look. I'm going to call the electrician and get this shit switched back to how we had it. And it's already passed inspection. So we're good?"

"We're good. Call me back and we'll get your power on." Mark was feeling for me; he knew I'd been taking the city's abuse for too long.

Needless to say, I was furious. Not only because I still didn't have lights on in my business and couldn't get any other inspections done until there was power, but more so because, had I not asked the question to Mark, the fucking lights would've have blown up and the city (inspector) would've have told me, "Tough luck... Not our problem," even though it would've been *entirely* their fault. I was about to lose it.

I walked toward the front of the building, down the dark hallway, to where a guy named Milo was working on finishing some drywall. (Milo was a pretty rowdy dude, a 300-pound L.A. Dodgers fan with a teardrop tattoo. That's not an exaggeration.)

"What's going on, Bryan?" Milo could tell I was fucking furious.

"Well, the power was hooked up wrong because of how the inspector insisted we wire it in order to pass, and if we would've flip the switch, all of the lights would've blown up." I was clearly worn out and ready to freak out, and Milo knew it.

"Well, look at it this way, Bryan. At least your lights didn't blow up," he offered with total sincerity.

I was stunned. I hadn't thought of it that way, and I was definitely not anticipating this simple but incredibly articulate, real-deal perspective to come from Milo. It was cool, and I was impressed.

"You know, that's a solid take. Great perspective. Thanks, Milo."

Milo was immediately proud of himself for this and went on to say, "Yeah. It's like the time they killed my brother."

"I'm sorry, what?" I honestly wasn't sure if I had heard that right.

"Yeah, they shot him in the back." Milo continued his insight. "And I was locked up. I told my homie I was going to *do* this motherfucker when I saw him on the inside. You know, kill him."

"Totally." I think that's what I said.

"But then my homie was, like, 'Milo, killing this motherfucker isn't going to bring your brother back. You know?'" Milo was nodding his head, and I was nodding along with him. "And I was, like, 'You're right.'"

"Yeah, that makes total sense. Thanks, Milo. Not killing your brother's murderer was a good call." As if I wasn't already scared of Milo, this took it to the next level.

Insight and perspective can come from the most unexpected places. And though I seriously do not think the decision to forego the revenge killing of your brother's killer because it won't bring him back is an apples-to-apples comparison to a construction mishap averted, I do still believe in and appreciate the perspective.

The power situation was a major issue that created very difficult setbacks throughout my project, but with perspective and endurance, the job went on and was completed. It can be difficult to see the forest through the trees at times, but if you think about the last "major" problem or setback you encountered, it is likely a challenge to recall, because you are on to solving the next and current major problem. It can seem daunting, but it's what you signed up for.

Eventually, the major problems and setbacks will subside, and business will go on as usual. Yes, stuff will break, employees will quit, and customers come with a whole new set of challenges, but with the experiences comes perspective, and thinking becomes a product of wisdom.

Thanks, Milo.

Takeaways:

- ✓ Perspective is a fuel.
- ✓ Revenge murdering your brother's killer doesn't help anyone.

###

CHAPTER 14

DOING SOMETHING FOR THE SAKE OF DOING IT

This Might Be the Last Chapter

TAKING A MINUTE to consider your motivation can give you a better understanding of your odds of being successful or of even finishing what you've started.

It is interesting to consider why people with incredible wealth continue to work on building more wealth. Motivation is subjective. There really isn't a right or wrong, for the most part. If you're looking to exterminate a particular part of the population because they are different from you, this is wrong. But when it comes to building businesses or wealth of any kind, there are typically fewer evil reasons for doing so.

Maybe your drive is to fill the bank account with as much cash as you can. Maybe you're into it for helping others or for helping others fill their pockets. Maybe it's the respect or power driving you to accomplish more. Regardless of your motivation, it is helpful to simplify this piece, in order to identify key drivers that will push the progress of your project and continue to motivate you to fight on.

I believe the best way to simplify the motivation is to consider *doing something purely for the sake of doing it.*

It won't be useful to apply this simplicity when working to secure a location or raise capital, but it can make all the difference when you're grasping for something to hold on to in the face of adversity. This is similar to Yvon Chouinard's take on setting a goal and then forgetting about it to just focus on the process, but it's pretty much the opposite of Simon Sinek's "Start with Why." Both mentalities have to be applied when and where appropriate.

Try to consider the necessity of pragmatism when you're in the shit and super-overwhelmed by the task at hand. If you're working towards raising the cash to get started, you cannot also be focused on the next locations and scaling the business, even if the big idea is to have the greatest impact possible. This is applicable to nonprofits just as much as it is to for-profit operations.

Sinek provides the Golden Circle through which to filter all your decision making, to ensure you remain on track with the heart of the movement or venture intact. But when you're *doing something for the sake of doing it,* it can be useful to just push forward to see how something is going to turn out. There's no time for delays, and, like my Uncle Dick says, "It's going to take you more time to think about all the ways something can get done than if you were to just fuck it up and redo it."

Too often, you will run into folks who want to tell you how something should be done, but you'll notice they haven't done anything, themselves. It is too easy to tell others what you would do rather than actually take action.

At the time of this writing, it is safe to say we are living in an over-coached society. You likely know what I'm talking about, but if you don't, I'm talking about the self-help industry and adult humans deeming themselves coaches and then trying to convince other adult humans they're going to benefit from the coaching. (This is much different than seeking a mentor with a proven track record of success, who will be eager to help you just in order to see you be successful.)

Unsolicited adult coaches are possibly one of the most stagnant, bullshit time-wasters you're going to come across. Not only is the arrogance of a weekend seminar they attended obnoxious, but their unfortified lack of experience is going to cost you time and money.

But wait: isn't this a self-help-type book? No. And if you picked it up in the self-help section or Amazon suggested it because you read *The Secret,* please let me know.

The point of pursuing anything is the experience of the pursuit; the fucking journey, not the destination. This is not going to be able to be explained to you (or coached) to the point where you go, "*Ah-hah!* That's so satisfying!" Coaching should be left entirely to sports; nothing to do with business. This is not a coaching book. It is just some lessons to consider as a way to mitigate disasters before they happen or as a reminder that you're not alone. I am about as qualified to coach someone on their life choices as I am qualified to deliver a child.

If you're in need of having someone tell you how to live your life, then do not start a business. If you're mental, see a trained professional psychologist or psychiatrist. If you're an addict or an alcoholic, then go to AA and find a sponsor.

Doing something for the sake of doing it can also relieve the pressures of working purely toward an end goal or result. Okay, consider this: most successful organizations created by people like Knight and Chouinard have a colorful history that began with a scrappy operation in pursuit of whatever got them to the next month, week, or even day, just trying to survive.

These now-titans of industry all look back on the good ol' days with a fondness that money cannot buy. If you maintain a devotion to *doing something for the sake of doing it,* then odds are you're going to be able to revel in that moment about the moments you're going to one day reminisce about. Be present for the whole experience, 'cuz you won't know it at the time, but the rough patches are sometimes the best of times. Get to the next step. The one after that will still be there.

Takeaways:

- ✓ The unknown is one of the big reasons people start businesses: to see what is going to happen.
- ✓ The adrenaline is a bonus.
- ✓ Talk about good stress in the "Born out of Necessity" chapter.
- ✓ Try to realize when you're in the best of times.

###

CHAPTER 15

HOW MANY *NOS* ARE LEFT IN THE NO BANK?

Plenty

A "*NO* Bank"? What the hell is a *NO* Bank?

Great question.

Hearing *NO* over and over again is going to be demoralizing, to say the least. But with the right mindset, the *NOs* can keep on coming and not even phase you. I like to think of the *NO* Bank as the number of times I can hear the word *NO* and keep going. To be clear: *NO* means No in some very particular situations. (This is not written by Harvey Weinstein.)

From the beginning and also discussed in Chapter 2, you'll hear the word *NO* in many forms when you're explaining your *crazy idea.* But the way the *NO* is expressed isn't necessarily going to be as clear as a plain sign of rejection; you might just get a look or a dismissal. The subtle *NO* is potentially even more damaging to your progress than when someone like your brother's neighbor comes out and just says, "That's not going to work." A subtle *NO* sneaks into your subconscious and plants a seed of doubt. The seed grows into a *NO* tree and then... Okay, I'll stop. You get it. Subtle *NOs* fuck up your motivation to go on.

However, with a simple formula, you don't have to worry about how many *NOs* you have left.

Arrogance + Stupidity = Anything is Possible

Kinda sounds like Forest Gump wrote a lyric for P Diddy, right?

It also sounds like self-help, but it's not. Arrogance is the uglier version of confidence, but if it means allowing you to not really give a shit about what someone else thinks about something you're pursuing, then why not?

There are plenty of regrets to be had, but it is often agreed the most festering regrets are also the regrets about attempts not made. Not giving a shit about what someone thinks of your idea isn't easy. But what about the people who are going to think your plan is awesome? Do they get a vote?

At every point in the project, there is likely going to be some form of opposition. It can even come from you just not knowing what the hell you're doing. Think about it. When you don't know how to do something or even what to do, it's like getting a *NO*, and stopping seems like the most logical step, the path of least resistance.

But rather than accept the fact that you don't know how to do something as a road block, falling back on arrogance to get it done is totally reasonable. In almost every single job interview I have ever done, I dish out the same line of bullshit: "There is plenty I don't know how to do, but there hasn't been anything I haven't been able to learn." (Feel free to borrow that.)

But it's true. Okay, it's mostly true, and I like to lean on it as a way of pushing forward to get shit done. Everything you currently know how to do had to be learned at some point. Imagine if your parents were trying to teach you how to walk, and you were, like, "No, that's okay. I don't know how to do that, so I think I'm going to just crawl through life." Arrogant babies?

And the stupidity part of the equation? What about that?

Being stupid isn't so bad as long as you're willing to try. Stupidity, as in the fact you don't know what you're doing, but that doesn't really matter, because you're going to find out. Stupidity is like a bottomless *NO* Bank. Hearing the word *NO* when you're stupid doesn't have the same effect.

Think about teenagers. Good listeners, staying inside the lines, being where they're supposed to be, and following all the rules. Nope. On an aggregate, they're fairly stupid as a group. (It's remarkable I wasn't dead before I turned twenty.) But we were all teens at some point. And before we were told we couldn't do something, we believed we could or just didn't give a shit if things didn't work out—we'd just try again. Allow stupidity to cast the consequences aside, because what would you attempt in a world where it didn't matter if it didn't work out?

But wait, Bryan. That's really stupid. And your fictional arrogant baby and dumb teenager world is not reality. I have a shit ton to lose, so what the fuck are you talking about?

I couldn't agree more and see your point 100 percent. But the reality is this is not the only piece of the puzzle necessary to accomplish the goal you've set out to accomplish. It is a combination of a number of different aspects that come together to give you the best chance at making it happen.

Again, this not a self-help book, but you cannot only roll on Chapter 12 without considering Chapter 5. If you're reading this and thinking, "Fuck it. Let's live for today and that's all we need," then you're a little too stupid. You still need to plan; you have to research, educate, identify, and anticipate risk, control every variable you possibly can. But do it with the mindset that you're *going* to survive this. Even your own *NOs* that surface from the years of conditioning to not rock the boat and the deep-seeded prefrontal cortex voice in your head that's always doubting you cannot stop you. *That's* the take necessary to decide you *can* hear the word *NO* a thousand times and still refuse to quit.

Feeling redundant? Well, it should. This non-self-help self-help book is meant to drill in the message of endurance. You're going to want to quit—everyone wants to quit. But the difference between those who quit and those who don't is simply the thousand-*NOs* mindset.

Want an example of hearing *NO* and not accepting it?

The first location for my Easy Float business was challenging enough, but it was still more difficult to secure a second location. The landlords of the ideal space for the second location were not interested in entertaining the concept, even though the modality of flotation was gaining serious momentum and had been championed by a number of key influencers, like Steph Curry, Tim Ferris, the Navy SEALS, and more. My real estate broker wasn't going to bat for me, either: these are the emails we exchanged, verbatim.

Jay:

Thanks, Bryan.

Like we discussed on the phone, the owners of the Box Factory aren't interested in the use.

Me:

Hey, thanks Jay.

I totally get the Box Factory isn't interested in the float concept, but I'm probably going to keep asking about it.

Jay:

We also heard back from the listing brokers for the Shops @ Boyd Acres. Your use is not going to be a fit.

Me:

Box Factory guys come around yet?

Jay:

The owners of the Box Factory haven't done a 180 on their decision, but we'll let you know if they do.

Me:

That's pretty funny, I'm still holding out for the 180!

This game of cat and mouse went on for some time, and I fully understood there was little chance of being successful in getting the location I was going for, but there was absolutely *ZERO* chance of being successful if I didn't at least try.

There is a line here that you don't want to cross. You absolutely have to be a squeaky wheel and also be willing to get a little awkward while not accepting the *NO*. But be aware that guys like Jay don't have time to waste and will quickly drop you, if they feel you're not worth their time. On the other hand, if your real estate person isn't going to bat for you in the first place, I'd suggest pushing it. You don't have the property to lose, so might as well go for it.

The book *Never Split the Difference: Negotiating as if Your Life Depended On It* by author and former FBI lead international kidnapping negotiator Chris Voss, provides practical but counterintuitive strategies and tactics to improve persuasion and increase your odds of being successful in negotiations. One of the nine strategies Voss heavily emphasizes and relied on is endurance.

Hanging in there sounds obvious, but it is more than that. For the endurance tactic to transcend into actual effective strategy, it takes more than hanging in there. Your level of poise in the most strangely awkward environments will determine whether or not you or the counterpart will concede first. Get comfortable with long, awkward pauses, and you'll start to see a difference immediately... eventually.

Never Split the Difference is a much better book than this one, and I highly recommend everyone read it a couple times and keep a copy close by for reference. Voss not only goes over strategies behind hostage negotiations, but he goes into depth on real-world applications, both in business negotiations and personal.

###

HERD

"It's not your fault, Will."

–Robin Williams, *Good Will Hunting*

TAKE ME SERIOUSLY. The Post-Industrial Revolution is to blame.

Notice how uncomfortable it is to step outside the lines of conformity. We're much safer within the herd, like the walrus in the center of a blubbery pack when a hungry polar bear approaches. Yes: **walruses** are indeed collected in a **herd**! (They can also be collected in a "pod" or a "huddle.")

If you're not outside the lines then the risk of failing or being torn to shreds by an artic predator decrease significantly. So yeah, it is semi-instinctual in terms of survival, but the amygdala aside, you/we have been conditioned for more than a century to not color outside the lines. When we hear the word *NO,* either externally or internally, we tend to listen. To avoid the risks.

Going against the conventions of societal norms is not easy and can be downright dangerous, but the first step in addressing the fact that you're weird is admitting it. Weird means you're willing to try to start your own business, even though society tells you not to. I mean Al Gore thinks he invented the Internet—what the fuck is that about?

So back to the Post-Industrial Revolution point, the Post-Industrial Revolution is a period in American history when we took people off the farms and put them in factories. How do factories work? Through systems, processes, and consistencies. I like systems, processes, consistencies as long as I am the one creating and/or applying them.

So, how do factories run? With the well-trained laborers on the machines. In order to ensure the laborers supported the processes, systems, and consistencies, it was vital to properly train and condition the workers. How to properly train/condition them? Refine and formalize early education to support the creation of the next set of workers. Put them at a desk and teach them to show up on time and fit in. Simple.

The entrepreneur is going to reject this wholeheartedly. Maybe not wholeheartedly in the beginning, but they will break free from the conventions of "normal" society and press on. It's not your fault, but if we want to point fingers… I guess Henry Ford is to blame?

###

CHAPTER 16

OTHER PEOPLES' SUGGESTIONS

Might be a Glimpse into the Near Future

THIS MIGHT BE A LITTLE premature. It was hard for me to decide if this was even an appropriate topic to discuss and/or challenge to include in this book or whether it may be a better fit for the sequel. I thought I was pretty sure the "Other Peoples' Suggestions" part of this journey was only applicable once your business was open and operating. But actually, even though you definitely suffer a greater amount of exposure to Other Peoples' Suggestions once you open your doors, you can save yourself a lot of post-decision heartache if you keep this concept in mind during the building and development phases, too.

If you're not great at making decisions, then I suggest you write *"Get better at making decisions"* on the inside cover of your notebook. (There are a few things to write on the inside covers of your notebook, but we'll get into that in a few chapters.)

Making decisions becomes exhausting quickly when you're creating your own concept and your own brand. Doing it is a little less tiresome when building a franchise, but you will absolutely still have to be comfortable making decisions, and usually without all the information you need or much time to contemplate. This is where I suggest re-reading Simon Sinek's *Start With Why* and, if you haven't already, writing your own *WHY*. Get your core values written inside the cover of your notebook, too, as soon as you know what they are. The reason it is important to get comfortable with making decisions and knowing what it is you're going for is because **<enter other peoples' suggestions here>.**

It is so easy for folks to say, "You know what you should do…?" But how is it the same people with all those outstanding ideas aren't doing anything with them, other than giving them to you? I don't mean to sound snarky or rude at all here. These folks are likely outstanding people who care about you and want to see you be very successful, but even with the best intentions, their advice can quickly turn your vision into soup at a potluck. People don't like soup at a potluck.

Think about it. You're going to a potluck, and you're ready to bring your favorite dish—let's say it's those enchiladas you're known for. Sounds like a good move. Can't go wrong. But then your neighbor drops in and is, like, "You know what I like? Carrots. Throw some carrots in the dish and *then* you've got something."

Then the roommate walks through the kitchen and says, "People at potlucks really like deviled eggs. You should do *that.*"

Next, you get a text from your dad. He wants to know what you're up to and then makes sure to tell you to consider turning it into a tortilla soup and, also, that not everyone likes cheese.

Lastly, your boyfriend calls and asks why it isn't going to be the brownies he really likes. But he reminds you he likes the enchiladas, too.

Now, is anyone going to strap on an apron and help you make the dish? Probably not. And when it goes wrong, even the most empathetic supporters might tell you what you should've done.

Going down the road of trying to make everyone happy is going to turn your vision into a Mexican carrot deviled egg soupy brownie, and no one wins.

When you're tired and overwhelmed by everything that still needs to get done, this is when your decision-making advice filter can weaken and bad shit can happen.

The endurance piece of the puzzle is critical in every way, when you're putting it all together. There is still going to be one hundred things you would've done differently, when it's all said and done, but keeping a little energy in the reserves so you can make the best possible effort to avoid saying, "Fuck it. Just do it however you'd do it," to a subcontractor, will make a major difference when you step back and see what you've made.

Gently and graciously accepting suggestions along the way is not the same as implementing those suggestions. No need to shut down people and hurt feelings, though. Practice saying "Thank you," and "Oh, that's a cool idea"; you're going to have to entertain lots of suggestions once your doors are open.

Sometimes, the suggestions are great and you should consider implementing some ideas. I have a rule of threes: once I hear the same suggestion three times, then I force myself to really consider how I can make it work, without entirely changing the business. Some folks want your lemonade stand to also fix smart phones! Wouldn't that be cool?

My lawyer, Spencer, is deaf and also the man. He started a business with an altruism backbone called the Smile and Nod Company. They make apparel and donate a big chunk of the proceeds to the deaf and hard of hearing community. Spencer tells me that's what people do when they can't hear you: smile and nod. Anyway, the point is, whenever I get the "You know what you should do...?" I just smile and nod.

When the public's expectations and your vision begin to align, that is when you know you've got something that is going to click.

I am a stubborn person. Most self-employed people are. This is the other side of the coin. Have you ever met a super-rude business owner and thought, *What the fuck is her deal?* Well, she probably has gotten worn down after nonstop, "You know what you should dos." It's easy to want to give the finger to anyone offering ideas after you've just gone through hell to make your dream a reality, but that's not the best business practice. Besides, consider if you made a business that is only just right for you, it would probably be weird.

It's a balance of having a desire to improve and grow and learn, and having thick enough skin to not freak out on the next person that says, "You know what you should do...?"

Notebook

I've mentioned a notebook a couple of times. I am a huge believer in writing stuff down—big surprise. But I'm not the only one who thinks this is a good practice. (It also makes people feel really important and appreciated, when you write something down they've suggested.)

The notebook I prefer fits comfortably in my back pocket, the cheapo-version Moleskin, and I have a $4 pen that fits in my wallet. I constantly write down ideas for improving the operations. I do not write "to-do" lists. It is commonly agreed this is a misuse of time and energy, as you will spend more time writing things down than just doing shit as it comes to you and needs to be done (Tim Ferriss methods). And if you have something buried behind two or three pages, its level of importance is pretty well indicated by the other items on top of it.

Your notebook serves another purpose, as well: write down your core values on the first page and the last page.

Unlike your business plan, the core values you develop need to be kept close and in sight.

A business plan is more of an exercise than anything else, to reveal the elements of the strategy you would not have otherwise thought of. But your core values are the beginning and the end of everything you're going to do. It doesn't mean the core values won't evolve, too. But they're going to come in handy when you need a reminder to keep it real. You've already envisioned how you want things to be. Remain dedicated to what is most important to you, as the suggestions come rolling in.

Our Core Values

1. Easy Float is for Everyone
2. It's not for everyone, and we're okay with that
3. We'll still have a beer with you
4. Know who we are
5. Simplify

The Serenity Now Limited core value that makes me the most frustrated—but also keeps me the most honest—is this: "Floating is for everyone." My staff has repeated this back to me I don't know how many times. It's always some jackass without any regard for the business or the facilities or the people working here who drives me to want to just forget Core Value #1 altogether... Or it's a white person with dreads.

It's always a white person with dreads...

The "you know what you should do!" section of this book was inspired by the unsolicited advice of a pair of life coaches.

Stick to your guns, and start to become okay with having shit fucked up because it was your fault. There is nothing worse than not being able to be the person responsible for a loss. Kinda similar to playing tennis, according to a pastor I know. In doubles, you have someone else to blame, but when playing singles, the outcome is all yours. It is much preferable to own the accountability rather than have to regret the advice you knew you shouldn't have taken.

There is a time when other people's suggestions can blur between someone attempting to convince you to fix a problem you don't have and someone actually identifying a problem you didn't realize. We're sensitive people, that's just our nature. And our business is like our child or dog. I have the absolute worst dog on the planet, and I'll be damned if anyone is going to say a bad word about him. But the fact of the matter is sometimes we all are a little too sensitive, and this can be a downfall; hopefully not *the* downfall.

We have a tendency to immediately reject other people's mere suggestions when they are suggesting that there may be a problem. This is yet another balancing act, and I do realize the contradiction I've made. I'm not talking about the life coaches out there who want to dish advice along with a side of smug. Rather, I mean the actually very proven and successful people who have been there before and might be exceptional at identifying an opportunity for improvement. There is a stark contrast between the coaches and the successful/proven entrepreneurs. (Look for my next book: *Why I Think Life Coaches are Idiots!* Just kidding, Dan.)

So, here's the value in the suggestions: acknowledge the possibility that there could be a problem *first*! And then address it.

I don't mean to address a problem by attempting to justify/deny that there even is a problem. But consider the solutions and think about trying them on for size. You don't want to miss an opportunity to receive sound critical feedback from a trusted and reliable source. There is always a time for the justify/deny method in appropriate circumstances.

###

CHAPTER 17

WHAT'S YOUR UNFAIR ADVANTAGE?

You're Going to Want to Get One

BY NOW, IT MIGHT FEEL like you're wondering what's the point? Is this all really worth doing? That nine-to-five where you leave it all at the office and have a 401k is sounding not so bad, and the security of that route is looking real nice.

Keep reading. It isn't all pessimism and misery. There is more satisfaction in it than just the satisfaction of surviving. This isn't the *Naked and Afraid* show! This is actually worth doing.

The previous paragraph is not really directly related to the Unfair Advantage, but it is kind of. The Unfair Advantage is part of why taking the risks and enduring is all worth it.

Figuring out what gives you a real competitive advantage is extremely satisfying, and then putting it into motion is what makes everything work and makes the whole process worth it. But you have to have a competitive advantage, and this doesn't necessarily mean something as blatant as, "We deliver and they don't."

It can be something exceptionally subtle, like controlling overhead to the point where your volume can remain lower and more manageable, to provide a better experience to every guest without having to charge a premium. This method should obviously develop into an increase in volume, but then you have the luxury of providing more staff to continue to provide the next-level experience. But does it sound like your unfair advantage is customer service, in this example??

Nope.

If any business ever tells you their customer service is what sets them apart from all the rest, they are stupid. Your customer service alone is not enough to make the difference, and every company wants to feel like they have outstanding customer service. This isn't as simple as telling the staff to do a good job and be nice. This is rooted in the corporate culture and company values. We'll get more into culture later on. The unfair advantage is the company's ability to run lean and ***still*** deliver an outstanding experience. Control the variables that you can, and demonstrate culture every day.

So, it's values and culture: *that's* the unfair advantage? Got it.

Not exactly. Though very important, the values and culture of a company are not the same as an unfair advantage. Think of an unfair advantage as something like finding a niche. Then being special in the niche, and then exploiting being special. Didn't people always tell you you were special?

Okay here.

"Almost anything can be copied. In fact, I'd claim that **anything of any value *will* be copied.** It should be part of your *business plan* that other people will copy you."

—Jason Cohen, founder of WP Engine,
Smart Bear Software

Cohen writes on in a series of blog post to support the evidence of what is *not* a competitive/unfair advantage and then goes even further to respectfully explain in the comments. He writes:

"No, I don't believe 'passion' or 'love' is an advantage. That is like saying 'love conquers all.' It's necessary but not sufficient, and for certain kinds of companies, it's not even necessary.

"I would agree that persistence can be an advantage. Sticking it out through the crap, going out and asking for what you need, and being willing to wade through years of crap to get to the end.

"Still, it's not enough, because you should assume your competition has that, too. Enough of them will."

The point Cohen is making is there has to be something more about what it is you do. There are too many exceptional people who are willing and dedicated to advancing a project or movement forward. There has to be something more.

There are so many ambitious people who will fail. But that doesn't mean it isn't worth trying. Rather, try to discover your own underbite thing and be willing to pick up the mike, next time you're at a karaoke bar.

https://blog.asmartbear.com/not-competitive-advantage.html

https://www.inc.com/karl-and-bill/what-is-your-unfair-advantage.html

From successful entrepreneur and angel investor Joshua Baer:

Here are a bunch of (not) competitive advantages I've seen:

we're enthusiastic!

we have having passion!

we are going to work harder than everyone else

we're built in the cloud (I put this one in an OtherInbox deck once)

we're students so we know the student market (replace "student" with anything)

we're going to charge less money *(I hear this so often)*

it's going to be just like XXX but we're going to let people do YYY

we're very, very excited!

None of these are real competitive advantages. You're better off just saying that you don't have any significant competitive advantages at this time and focus on why that's not as important in your situation or how you plan on acquiring competitive advantages.

Most startups don't have any significant competitive advantages (besides being a startup). You don't have to have a competitive advantage to succeed. But competitive advantages reduce risk and that's why investors are trained to look for them.

http://www.austinpreneur.com/when-does-a-competitive-advantage-matter-most/

So! I have gotta offer up at least a few possible unfair competitive advantages. Ours has always been the "run lean" option. None of these suggestions are new or innovative in a way that a unique unfair advantage will exist in your outfit. They are more like a framework or system to work with.

- ➢ **Simplify**
- ➢ **Lean**! Of course, that's number one. I am a huge fan of the bootstrappers out there.
- ➢ **Inside Info**. Of course, not like the insider-trading-type info, but, rather, you know something the others don't.
- ➢ **Being the first!** This is a very tricky unfair advantage because you're paving the way for the competition to learn from your mistakes and ride the momentum you've created. Nevertheless, you get to capture as many followers as you can first and set the bar, then keep the bar notching up.
- ➢ **Being second!** Yeah, that's an advantage too, 'cuz you're not going to have to take the licks the first guy did. But you have to exploit the hell out of this. Being third doesn't mean shit as far as advantages go.

###

CHAPTER 18

THIS BOOK WAS WRITTEN IN 40 DAYS

'Cuz Otherwise it Would have Never Gotten Done

ADMITTEDLY, IT IS RECKLESS to write a book in forty days, especially one you think people should read and take stuff away from. But I wrote it in forty days for a couple of reasons.

One: Writing a book in forty days meant it had to get done; being accountable to a time constraint prevents procrastination. There are lots of talented writers out there with okay books still floating around up in their heads.

Two: I don't have time to wait. Just like in building a business, **there is no time to not do something**. So many people talk about what they want to do rather than just doing it.

The simplest way to look at anything is: "If you don't do it, it will not happen."

###

CHAPTER 19

CULTURE

In the Beginning and the End

SINCE THIS BOOK IS intended to examine the earlier stages of company development, I won't go too far into demonstrating values in operations, but it is important to develop values for your business early on in the process. This can circle back to your *WHY* and core values. It's something important to have on hand always. It is also important to realize there is an inevitable evolution of values that you hope will be subtle.

When you inevitably hear from someone—probably in the finding capital phase—you have nothing in your business idea or plan, that's when you lean on your core values and your culture. These nay-sayers are not wrong: technically, you *don't* actually have anything truly tangible—no numbers to support the business, other than really nice-looking cash flow projections supported by thorough research. But, on the other hand, they're kinda wrong. You have a vision along with the business' initial structure and your personal drive to make it all come together.

How you respond to the endless adversity that comes with creating anything will be directly reflected in your culture. Demonstrate the business culture you want to cultivate. This is not something that can be faked: the culture piece has to be authentic if it has any chance of standing up to future corruption.

Opportunities to demonstrate your values come at you quick (and don't worry if you fuck it up; you're human), but this is the real-deal time to see how authentic your company's values truly are. It'll likely be an interaction with a contractor or a customer/guest. It's your culture and your values, so only you know how you'd prefer to be received. But if you're into the Stoic Philosophy or you're reading *The Guide to the Good Life* or the *Book of Joy*, then maybe you're practiced enough to pause in a difficult interaction, Zach Morris-style, and select the reaction that best reflects your values.

Your core values are unlike the business plan exercise. Business plans are essentially useful until you actually open; they are a great way to uncover and reveal parts of your enterprise that are missing. The core values, however, will ride with you till the end. I believe it's useful to have five. And no more than five.

Easy Float's Core Values (again)

1. The Absolute Best Float Experience for Everyone
2. It's not for everyone and that's okay
3. But we'll still have a beer with you
4. Know who we are
5. Simplify

Super corny? Sure. But they're mine, and they help me craft a culture that's been not just well received but has kept me sane many times. And when I heard, "You don't have anything," I said, "Yeah, I do."

###

CHAPTER 20

THE THING WE BUILT AND IT'S HERE

...or the Thing we Pissed a Ton of Money Away on Ten Years Ago

BY NOW, HOPEFULLY, YOU'VE realized you have to be at least somewhat comfortable with risk and at least a little excited about the unknown to start a new business. 'Cuz that's how it is: you cannot predict the future and that's what's coming.

It helps to have others going through similar struggles with you at the same, not only to learn from, but to commiserate with and lend perspective. My friend Paul is credited with the subtitle on this chapter, and I have held the idea pretty close throughout the adventure. But it is 100% true: you don't know if whatever it is you're working on will have the stamina or structure or whatever it needs to sustain the next decade of tests that the market is going to throw at it. But the big question is do you do it anyway?

If you're the type who would rather work hundred-hour weeks working for yourself and make $50,000, rather than make $90,000 working for someone else, then there's your answer. You're running down the opportunity for the experience with the hope it is all going to click and be embraced like the Macy's Thanksgiving Day Parade. There are no guarantees. One more time: there are *NO* guarantees. And it makes a major difference when you're trying to sleep at night, so please, get really comfortable with this reality.

But you know what? If you're the person choosing the $50k, your mentality is already on the fuck-it side: it's just money, and you're not dead; you can always just make some more, if you're willing to.

I told my wife, even if everything went to shit and I lost everything, I would just buy a Geo Metro and get a couple of jobs, one working at night, sweeping and mopping at the Burger King down the road. She's a very lucky girl.

Telling yourself you can't do it or you just need a couple more things to get started is the same as getting a *NO* and accepting it. You will never be entirely ready to make something happen. If you ever say, "I want to do that," then you're probably not going to do it. It starts with movement. To clarify: saying *"you want to"* versus *"I'm doing this,"* is the mental point I'm trying to get at. How many times have you heard someone hear another person's idea or plan and say they want to do it?

Get comfortable with the fact that everything will go away at some point, and the risk of the unknown becomes a shadow of a doubt rather than a giant fucking monster in the closet. Think about your own risk tolerance and the impermanence in everything. Get comfortable with idea that things can also not work out, but the sting of failure is less than the sting of regret. When my friend first made the comment, *ten years ago, that our venture into this industry could be a thing we pissed away a ton of money on*, I kicked my head back, laughing, and was relieved to hear I wasn't the only one thinking that. But it's okay.

I understand going all-in means something different for everyone; everyone's parachute is different. I'd challenge, though, that the entrepreneur **without** a trust fund is at a unique advantage, as opposed to the rich kid.

Think about it. We've all been guilty of procrastinating, but when your back is against the wall, do you get it done and make it work? Or fold and say it doesn't matter because... (fill in the blank)? Besides that, when you have nothing to lose, it puts the risk in perspective. Just buy a Geo Metro, get back to work, save up a little money, and go at it again. Somewhat off the focus of choosing to not do something, because there's no guarantee it will be around in the future, but this is still a mindset.

This is all a tough pill to swallow. It's almost like thinking, if you make it to the other side, will it still even matter? That's why you don't open a froyo franchise. It makes a difference to try to double Dutch your timing into whatever industry you're betting on, but identifying a home run is far from easy. If you can catch something in its infancy or on the resurgence, most concepts remain cyclical, like real estate, that's ideal. But it doesn't have to be the perfect step in the right direction to be worth it. Just keep going.

Think of it as the regrets concept: the sting of failure is a lot less painful than the regret of not knowing how it could've gone. Or how about all the times you or anyone has thought or said, "I should've bought a house over in that part of town," but you didn't, because it was risky and you didn't know what it would be worth in ten years. It's the same thing. You don't know, but *no one* really does. Just don't be the last guy to the table.

Hindsight bias is looked at in depth in Nassim Nicholas Taleb's book, *Fooled by Randomness*. The bias can be seen largely in journalists' impressions and conveyance of the success and the road to success of very successful people. Simply, the successful person made all the right moves, but the bias enters with the journalists' disregard for the all the potential alternative outcomes, because there are too many variables to measure. One event out of place could create an entirely different outcome, and the successful person could be a failure or average. They wouldn't look so brilliant if the pieces hadn't come together. It's a book based off the movie *Butterfly Effect* staring Ashton Kutcher. No, that isn't right; but it's kinda the same idea.

But here's the deal: *you don't know you're making the wrong move while you're making it, and making no moves at all can still be the wrong thing to do.* You cannot possibly control all variables to make the absolute perfect outcome and become successful. It's all random and nothing matters; however, keep going, because there is meaning in what you're doing. Be okay with not knowing the outcome.

###

CHAPTER 21

BORN OUT OF NECESSITY

Better or Worse, Who Cares?

I HAVE TALKED A LOT about bootstrapping and may have over-romanticized the concept. Bootstrapping is the furthest thing from romantic. When you're on your hands and knees, hacking a shower pan, or breaking your back moving concrete, you will not be thinking of roses and champagne. One person even said to me, "You know there's some things you just have to pay for." *But how the fuck do you pay for something without money?*

Exactly. It doesn't matter. And if you begin to feel sorry for yourself, it's the beginning of the end. You signed up for it.

The subtitle on this chapter is the explanation in its most simple form: it doesn't matter. Would it be nice to have a blank check? Duh. But that's not the reality, so it doesn't matter which is better. It only matters that it gets done.

Consider a scenario where money isn't the solution to the problem. Let's say the problem is a space constraint by a window and a narrow stairwell. What then? Turn and walk away from the perfect lease and perfect location? Or do you build the equipment you need and make the best of it.

And when you've survived this bootstrapping stage and you're on to the next thing, it really doesn't matter how you got to the next step because the next steps will likely also require the bootstrapping methods. Put it in the core values or title your business plan, *Never Quit & And Just Keep Going*.

"Don't Stop."

—Phil Knight

This isn't to say that bootstrapping as a strategy is the same as "born out of necessity." Controlling variables and doing everything you can to maintain the lowest startup cost possible without directly compromising the brand/company's image and end-consumer experience is intelligent strategy. *Non-motivating* stress from having to "make something work" isn't a strategy, but it is a necessity. It's important to highlight the difference.

I've explained a number of decisions I made with the phrase "born out of necessity." It's not exactly how I wanted to do it, but it is the way it had to be done in order to move on to the next steps. Looking back on the grit demanded of you when your back was against the wall is satisfying and educational, but you will be fairly pissed in the moment. But that's why we have beer.

Avoid comparing your budget with others'. Wishing you had something does nothing except waste time and slow progress. "If I only had this, then..." Nope. That's the same thing people think and say who never start anything and definitely aren't completing anything. Refusing to accept the circumstances as defeat will make the difference.

You are likely in a phase, or have been in the phase, or soon will be, of *"Do whatever it takes to get the shit done."* Tough pills to swallow, but you will seriously be able to revisit every duct-taped part of the puzzle later on down the line, when you're bringing in the cash to correct or improve whatever you did to get open. Here is an opportunity to compartmentalize the project and put pieces into categories or parts, to try to reign in a massive undertaking and make it manageable. **Parts and phases**. You'll probably have a few different job titles, all simultaneously, and when one thing gets jacked up in one of your "jobs," it's still manageable. If two "jobs" have crises, then you're going to feel it. When all three jobs have fires to put out? Well, you're kinda fucked. Give Larry a call and let him have it.

No, you're still good. Break it down into parts, and prioritize. It's unlikely the problem won't still be there tomorrow for you to solve.

Again, bootstrapping and necessity in the moment are not enjoyable conditions. Most people will give up. The entitled don't even get a chance to give up.

There's a good type of entitlement, however. Another mindset cue, but if you only see the outcome as being one of success, you can consider yourself entitled to said outcome. Entitled is not enough to make a pie; you're going to need several ingredients. And, frankly, you don't have to be entitled to get the pie baked. But if you are, then I suggest making the attempt to be the kind of entitled that gets shit done, because you don't see why they shouldn't be getting done.

Expect the win.

The types of entitled: that's actually a nice segue into the *humble & hungry* idea. Write it down.

In my experience, I have been fortunate to have several outstanding influencers in my professional life. One told me, "Don't kill yourself. They're just jackets." (Tom Trissel) And another actually kept a piece of paper with the words *humble and hungry and something else* printed out at his desk. It wasn't like a motivational poster on the wall behind him, reminding him of the importance of team work or what it means to soar like an eagle. It was a plain sheet of paper, and it only had three words printed on it: Humble, Hungry, and Something else. (I can't actually remember the third word, and I kinda prefer that way.) Fill in the blank. User's-choice-type of a deal.

The dude nailed it with two words, not to mention he was a very intelligent person with a willingness to teach. He also coined the phrase, "Are you asking me or telling me?" (Alex Frio) But that's a much better lesson to include in the sequel.

Humility can be easily lost when you're focused on ambition or the *hungry* piece. And this is really the excellence in the simplicity of the two words: they require balance. And the *something else* is just as crucial—I understand it's cold to do that to you, and I apologize, but the *something else* is the interchangeable key element to the individual and the unique success of not only changing circumstances, but also the

151

incredibly unique circumstances of everyone's different project.

Be entitled to what it is you're killing yourself to create, and stay humble and hungry along the way. Easy as pie.

Eventually, you stop seeing it any other way. What I mean is the tasks in front of you, whether you can or cannot afford them, will have to get done, and you're the person responsible for getting them done. It's almost comparable to a flow state. You begin to act and react without having to think about what you're doing.

Rarely will this be an automatic, and if this is your first project, then hopefully you're going to develop the reflex to continue to build on the momentum.

Something useful in the beginning is to just ask out loud, "Well, how do we do this and what do we need to do next?" Often, someone standing in the room will assume the questions are directed toward them, and they might have the winning idea. If people just stare at you, then pretend it was a rhetorical question. Fake the confidence needed to get the job done. The fake confidence might morph into real confidence.

Once, someone asked if I was an engineer, and I was baffled. Why the fuck would you think I was an engineer? I can barely read!" But winging it turned nothing into something, and to someone looking in from the outside, they wouldn't have known the difference.

Think about that. No one knows you don't actually know what you're doing. It's like hiding in plain sight, if you just do the fake till you make it. I mean, if you're reading this, you're pretty deep into the book, and you've probably assumed I'm an author. I am about as much an author as I am an engineer. Which takes us to the critical factor in bootstrapping, called *winging it.*

Some of the most fun you're going to have on your journey will come from winging it. (Don't forget about all those impressive companies and their founding members who have fond recollections of the good ol' days, when they were barely holding on.) Winging it, with the exception of life safety, is not a bad move and often is the only move. Ask, "What's the worst thing that can happen?" If it's not death or pregnancy, then how bad could it be? Short term jail time. That's probably the worst. Try to avoid getting arrested, but consider the move Uber pulled in the beginning and continues to pull.

The DMV says Uber needs a permit to test its autonomous vehicles, but Uber argues that its vehicles aren't autonomous at all and therefore it doesn't need a permit.

"We respectfully disagree with the California Department of Motor Vehicles legal interpretation of today's autonomous regulations, in particular that Uber needs a testing permit to operate its self-driving cars in San Francisco," Uber's self-driving car lead Anthony Levandowski said in a statement to reporters.

https://techcrunch.com/2016/12/16/uber-continues-self-driving-vehicle-testing-in-sf-in-defiance-of-dmv/

The respectful defiance is a perfect example of doing what it takes and asking for forgiveness. Many self-starters are incapable of even considering the choice to not do something.

###

CHAPTER 22

SOMETIMES THAT NINE-TO-FIVE LOOKS PRETTY SWEET

The Other Side

THIS IS A TRAP.

I've heard, once you are self-employed, you're unemployable. And it is 100% true. So, know what you're getting yourself into before you make the transition, because there's no going back.

I would never go so far as to say that people working nine-to-fives for other people are wrong in any shape or form. I have nothing but respect and appreciation for anyone working a job; that includes telemarketers or the people out there cold-calling for anyone or anything—be kind to these people; they're working.

There are still days where I think about how nice it would be to have a boss. Someone to tell me what to do next. Someone to tell me what time to call it a day. Someone to approve the vacation time, so I know something isn't going to come up or an employee isn't going to bail without notice to jack up a beach trip I was looking forward to for months.

Here's the deal, though: you go to the other side, and there is no going back. I love it when I talk to entrepreneur friends who bitch about equipment breaking, a city official jamming them up, or an employee who positioned something on the floor to slip on, in order to collect disability (but they did it all on camera). They (we) love to complain about how rough it can get, but we always crack up at the end of the conversation, when they say something like, "Yeah, I'm going fishing" or "Headed to the airport—going to Hawaii," and it's a random Tuesday morning.

Separate note possibly for the next book: Do you run your business or does your business run you? I want to talk to you about automation and the Tim Ferris books.

The grass is greener because it is fertilized with bullshit.

Ever been fired?

I was fired from the last "real job" I had, and it wasn't cool. I'd been fired on one other occasion, but that was because I tried to glue a coworker to a toilet seat (and that's a whole other book).

The time I was unjustifiably fired from a job where I was working exceptionally hard to improve the company's positions and to support the team objectives was an entirely different experience. I was working in international development for a couple of footwear brands based in Portland, Oregon and was making the absolute best effort to be successful in my role with the company. Granted, I have never really been considered a company man by my peers, but I was still a person driven to put in my best work, no matter the circumstances.

I did everything to grow an under-supported international network through relationship building and was having a big impact on the brands' presence internationally. We were even able to acquire a key distributor in South Korea by pulling him away from a competitor. I was doing everything I could and not missing a beat. Then the international director was fired for reasons I wasn't privy to, but likely for no good reason at all, considering the company's reputation for axing good and dedicated people as if it were a normal thing to do.

I was bummed to see my director let go; I felt I could genuinely learn from him. Nevertheless, I found myself in the conference room with the CEO, CFO, Directors, and VPs, explaining the state of the international business. It wasn't a big deal to me, just doing my job, and I felt like it went well. After the meeting, I was walking back to my desk when the CEO stopped me and thanked me for my work. He told me, "This is a big opportunity for you," and I said, "Thanks. I'll do the best I can." And that was the end of my day.

About a week went by. I continued to manage the business as a one-man show on the International Team; the executive who inherited the role of temporarily supervising the one-man international team was a good guy and realized and acknowledged the amount of work and responsibility I had inherited. He showed a real appreciation for the work I had been doing. There was just one problem: *Mike.* I had a guy named Mike in a weird, still-kinda-my-supervisor position from the customer service roll I had transitioned out of. But once the international director was chopped, my fate, for some reason, rolled back into a previous supervisor's hands.

I should mention, I originally started with the company in the boot return room, where I was micromanaged for eight hours a day while taking shit-covered used boots out of boxes and placing them on a conveyer belt. I'm not too proud to do whatever it takes to get a foot in the door.

Mike sat next to me and observed the amount of work I was left to do solo on the international team. He told me I would be receiving a promotion and a raise and that it would be coming soon. My passport was ready and I was ready, too.

That Friday, Mike's co-manager, Stacy, approached me late in the afternoon. "Mike wants to see you in the conference room downstairs," she said.

"Okay. Do I need to bring anything?" I asked, having a suspicion.

"Nope," she chirped soullessly.

"So, Mike would like me to join him for an unscheduled meeting in the conference room downstairs at 4:30 p.m. on a Friday, and I don't need to bring anything?"

"Yep," replied Stacy.

Me: "Great. It's been real. Thanks."

When I walked into the conference room, Mike was sitting with the HR VP. I took my seat. Mike told me, "There's no easy way to say this, so we're going to have to let you go."

"Okay. Can you tell me why?" I was pissed and not about to let him off that easy.

"Well, you're just not a good culture fit." Oregon is a *right to work state,* so you don't actually have to have a reason to fire someone, which is actually a good thing in many circumstances.

"Well, it would be really helpful to me if you could be more specific, so I don't make the same mistakes in my next job." I was kinda serious, and he was turning red.

"No, I don't think we can go into it," said the coward.

"No, it's okay," offered our HR VP. "You can tell him why he's being let go." He was a really decent person with a very difficult job.

Mike went on to tell me there was a complaint about me, but he couldn't say from whom, and that he didn't like having to do this and all that shit. But then the HR VP had to excuse himself to go get me a severance check, that's when I just about made Mike cry.

"What's up, man? Why are you doing this?"

Mike said, "I don't like doing this. I feel sick to my stomach." He was turning red and trembling.

I go, "Yeah, that's your body telling you you're doing something pretty fucked."

The HR VP returned, and I walked with him to the parking lot with my stuff from my desk boxed up, which was waiting for me outside the conference room door. The little peckerhead of a dude who calls dibs on packing up other people's shit on these occasions likely got his jollies from loading my personal belongings into a cardboard box.

It was pouring rain. Portland. And then HR VP asked me if I needed and umbrella. I told him no thank you, that this felt about right.

I got into my Jeep and headed to the grocery store to grab a case of beer and go to a friend's apartment. Since they held on to my company phone, I got to just be alone with my thoughts, rather than make any breaking-the-news phone calls.

It was a decision-time-type moment.

I decided never to get fired again. The only way I could see not ever being fired again (especially without just cause) would be to make it so I was the only one who could fire me.

While there are still a lot of pros to working at someone else's company, there is never real security. It would be nice to leave your work at the office, but it isn't worth not being in the driver's seat when it comes to determining your own success and failure.

###

CHAPTER 23

WHAT IF IT WAS EASY?

Ask Yourself

IF STARTING YOUR NEW BUSINESS was easy, would you still do it? Would it even be worth doing?

It once again all depends on how you look at it. I met a psychic the other day, and she kept letting me know what her guides were telling her about my business. (Sorry, she was an intuitive, not a psychic.) I try not to shut this kind of stuff down, although I have in the past been that guy to call bullshit pretty quick. Rather, I want to take the opportunity to hear from a person that hears voices. Even if the voices are in their head, they still could provide valuable insight, and this person was excellent to talk with. Besides, we all have a voice in our head.

She told me the guides were telling her my place of business has good vibrations and the people are coming here for a reason. And that's true, even if they don't know why they came in the first place.

One thing that stuck out when talking to her was her story of a person who came to her asking why she had been diagnosed with cancer. Her response was, "Exactly. *Why you?*"

It's a technique intuitives use to create an illusion of intuition from another space. But, really, it just reemphasizes a different word repeated back to a person, the English-language intuition. But! That move can serve a purpose, too. Just by repeating a word back to the person, it offers a possible new perspective on their situation.

So, is it all worth it? Would it be worth it if it was *easy?*

Depends on your perspective.

(A Sequel to <u>Don't DO It!</u>)

This was my book's joke title originally, but there is something there, some merit to the validity of the statement. I, and I believe a number of other folks, would recommend not taking the plunge. Not by way of blatant discouragement, but, hopefully, more in a way to deliver a soft *NO* to kick off the trail of *NOs* to come. Not in a shitty or testing you type of way, but there is misery along with the satisfaction, and it certainly is not for everyone. Plus, remember, there is no going back once you go *unemployable*. What I mean by *going unemployable* is, once you work for yourself, there is no going back. Once you are your own boss, whether you fail or succeed, you will not be good at working for someone else.

If you're cut from the "be your own boss" cloth, then this thing is easy to brush off. If you're thinking you still may need time to think about whether this is the right path for you, then you're way more intelligent than most entrepreneurs ("do first, think later" types); keep giving the notion its due consideration and make a choice that makes sense for you and your family/lifestyle.

The last thing this book is intended for is to discourage anyone from taking off on something that everyone else says is impossible. It is a challenge worth accepting.

(A Prequel to <u>You DID It!</u>)

And here come the optimists! You will again drink beers in joyous celebration, not just as a way to move concrete solo. Celebrate along the way, too.

There are so many giant obstacles, but there are just as many opportunities for little celebrations. When I finally was able to submit my plans to the city (logging them in), my wife was thrilled for me. "You Did It!" And I was much less excited, only because I knew I was just getting started on the misery of plan review, but it did help me, hearing the excitement of a small victory. A big step forward deserves at least a mini-bottle of champagne or maybe a trip down to TGI Fridays—something.

The *BIG* "You Did IT!" is something to be celebrated (and it will happen—hang in there). But this is, yet again, another exciting beginning. Finding the thing you are excited about enough to build a business is tough. Turning that thing into an actual operating business is tougher. And actually making the business successful and sustainable is even tougher. Do not go, "If I build it, they will come," because, even if you are fortunate enough to have people find you, you still have to do everything you can to have enough of the right people like you. And you need them to tell others.

Your efforts continue and the job changes.

Is it Worth It?

Yes.

Keep your head up. You've heard this your entire life. If you strike out, keep your head up. If he or she shuts you down, keep your head up. If you don't get the job, keep your head up.

In an effort to not jump up onto the old soap box, I will refrain from going into why technology and a few decades of coddling has turned our society into a bunch of pussies. Instead, let's take another moment to focus on what it's all about:

✓ Perseverance
✓ Determination, and
✓ Endurance
✓ And other synonyms

The other night, my wife and I were watching *Shark Tank*. You're likely familiar with the show, if you're reading this. Sometimes, there are incredible stories of how entrepreneurs ended up on the carpet in front of the Sharks; "against all odds" types of stories, and stories of incredible sacrifice.

Many entrepreneurs have awesome back stories, but this particular pitch was pathetic, not because he had a terrible idea—it just wasn't ready. It was pathetic because every time a Shark would go out, he would drop his head and sulk. Every time!

It is understandable to be disappointed when you're so close and really want to make a deal. You feel you've put in the time and commitment. But if you're getting dished one *NO* after another by the Sharks, then the last thing you want to do is look like a bitch on national TV. He literally put his head down after every *NO*. Sulking.

The guy even turned back to make a last-ditch effort to convince the Sharks he deserved a deal. He told them about how hard he worked, coding in the back of the bus while traveling with his college basketball team, and he described the experience as if it was the same as taking shells in a basement in Aleppo. He was too proud of himself and believed he deserved something. He was promptly put in his place for patting himself on his own back. To make the circumstance even worse, the cameras showed him crying in the back room to his mother as she coddled him. It was absolutely brutal to watch.

Keep your head up. Even if you're making the mistake, don't make it worse by feeling sorry for yourself. There is no acceptable situation in which to feel sorry for yourself. And your posture makes a difference when you are feeling like the next *NO* is going to be your last. If you put your head down like a dog that just got caught in the trash, then you're going to feel sorry for yourself, because your posture is making you feel helpless and weak.

Here's some more info on that:

In a 2009 study published in the European Journal of Social Psychology, Petty along with other researchers instructed 71 college students to either "sit up straight" and "push out [their] chest" or "sit slouched forward" with their "face looking at [their] knees." While holding their assigned posture, the students were asked to list either three positive or negative personal traits they thought would contribute to their future job satisfaction and professional performance. Afterward, the students were asked to take a survey where they rated themselves on how well they thought they would perform as a future professional.

The researchers found that how the students rated themselves depended on the posture they kept when they wrote the positive or negative traits. Those who were in the upright position believed in the positive and negative traits they wrote down while those in the slouched over position weren't convinced of their positive or negative traits. In other words, when the students were in the upright, confident position, they trusted their own thoughts whether those thoughts were positive or negative. On the other hand, when the students sat in a powerless position, they didn't trust anything they wrote down whether it was positive or negative.

BUSINESS BOOKS AREN'T FUNNY

However, those in the upright position likely had an easier time thinking of "empowering, positive" traits about themselves to write down while those in the slouched over position probably had an easier time recalling "hopeless, helpless, powerless, and negative" feelings, according to Erik Peper, professor of psychology at San Francisco State University.

https://www.fastcompany.com/3041688/the-surprising-and-powerful-links-between-posture-and-mood

###

CHAPTER 24

STAYING HONEST WITH EVERYONE

Including Yourself

THIS IS A TWO-PARTER, and I swear this book will come to an end eventually.

Being honest with everyone is a fairly easy and achievable concept. *And* it makes a tremendous difference, when all is said and done. It can be a challenge to *not* cross your fingers behind your back when you're talking to the underwriter, but it is an even bigger challenge avoiding unwanted advances in the showers when you're doing time for fraud.

Now, there is a fine line, and there can come a time when you're going to have to ride this line, but here are a couple of techniques to keep you from crossing it. It's simple: don't say something that isn't true, and definitely don't email something untrue; this is the technique simplified. Think of it as a cousin to the "omission of the truth" idea, meaning not saying something is the same as lying in the dating world, but this isn't dating.

If you need more time to explain, then just shut up and take your time. "Can I get back to you? I'm not totally certain on that," is a totally acceptable and honest phrase for getting more time to remain honest and stay organized. Or even better, "I can't be entirely certain, but I think...," is another great phrase for keeping the conversation moving in the right direction, but with a disclaimer. Disclaimers work best when they are offered *before* they are required or requested, because, once they're requested, they're no longer a disclaimer; they become excuses and that's no good.

So, to dial it in on the First Part:

- ✓ Never write an email that has any form of dishonesty.
- ✓ And use disclaimers before making excuses.

Honesty 101. Kinda. The omission idea is a hot cousin you should avoid kissing.

Second part: Being honest with yourself is much different. There is real value in creating realistic expectations for yourself rather than lying about where you are in the process, especially about what you're actually going to be capable of in a time constraint. Think of compartmentalizing meets confidence meets reality.

It is no doubt a good thing to adopt a mindset where you have the belief and confidence of achievement and you stay unstoppable in your process. However, when you have to come to the cold grips of reality—say, when you thought you would have several locations in operations by the end of year one or several deals closed by the end of the week—it does you no good to get burned up by working to achieve what may be impossible and then take a punch after the bell, on top of that. Setting a well-considered goal with at least some potential for completion is a much more honest and healthy way to motivate yourself and drive progress.

Setting realistic expectations for yourself is easy, if you're not an entrepreneur. Chances are you have some big dreams, and I can go fuck myself. But hear me out. Similar to setting the goal and then focusing on the process, this is a way to set yourself up to avoid the burnout. You will still achieve, but this method increases the odds. Set benchmarks you *know* you will need to reach before moving to the next steps. Usually the next steps look like, "How are we going to scale?" We love to dream about scaling our business, but don't try to eat before you've set the table.

The second part of the second part pertains to knowing when something is fucked. It's much less enjoyable than setting goals and creating the processes to achieve them.

At some point in time, you are going to find yourself in a position where you will have to cut something loose, and, hopefully you have compartmentalized effectively. It is not necessarily a bad thing to be reminded you are human; it feeds the humble piece of the equation. It is a bad thing to find out your crazy idea, as a whole, was actually a really stupid idea and you just got your ass handed to you. Try to avoid this. But finding a piece of the overall whole that is not working out is not a bad thing. It actually leads to innovations and improvements. But, if you deny the fact or lie to yourself that something isn't working, then you're going to do way more harm than you would have, had you just cut it off.

SO many people use the word pivot. It's a term that surfaced from Silicon Valley fuckups (startups?), and it is a cowardly attempt to deny to yourself and others that something doesn't work. You're pretending you had it when you knew you didn't. The better and more respectable alternative is to own the error first and then adapt, rather than pivot. Accountability is cool.

###

BRYAN MESSMER

CHAPTER 25

DO NOT DAYDREAM

Sleep Dreaming is Okay

IS THIS ANOTHER CHAPTER where Bryan contradicts something written previously in the same book? Not exactly, but I understand the tone.

Dreams are good. Having dreams are better. Setting out on a committed path to achieve your dreams with a mindset and a plan to support the endurance required is the best.

Day dreaming, however, is very bad and will cost you something you will not get back. Time.

We all do it. The zoning out, thinking about what if someone just rolled up and threw a big bag of sweet cash at you and then you'd be set to take the risks or you'd have the last piece to a puzzle you haven't even started. Or, randomly, you're going to meet someone who knows the buyer, and they're going to love you and your idea, and then they're going to buy and you're going to be rich! And then you're going to get to go to a sweet party where Jack White performing, just randomly, and he's going to be all, like, "Aren't you that guy? And do you want to play the drums for the next set?" And then you do! Even though you've never taken a single lesson on playing drums in your Life! And then!

I'll stop. But you can see how much time this wasted, when I should've been working on the next email campaign to drive revenue, increase brand awareness, and further develop my business. You do not have time to day dream, and if you want to play the drums, it's never too late, as long as you're not lazy.

Make the call.

This entire chapter(book) could be retitled *You're Procrastinating: WHY are You Procrastinating?*

There's no reason to continue distracting yourself, and there's no reason to not try something. Now Go Do Something.

###

CHAPTER 1

IT'S NEVER FINISHED

Embrace the Work-in-Progress

THIS IS NOT A MISTAKE. This is the actual Chapter One. If you take anything away from this book, rip this page out and fold it up and keep it in your pocket.

If you're like most entrepreneurs, you're kinda obsessive and have an unstoppable drive to create, and you likely suffer from an inability to be satisfied with your own work.

I only wish someone would have told me this.

Your project/business/whatever/book will never, ever be truly complete.

It'll get done, but it won't be done to you. Everyone will tell you how excellent it is and that you've done a great job and their pats on the back and congratulations will give you a fleeting sense of accomplishment. You're going to need a good hard slap to the face (figuratively) to make you realize that you did a good job. But *still* not good enough, for you. That's the combination that keeps you tinkering and creepily unhappy with how things look, knowing they could always be better.

And that's just it. They can *always* be better, so you're going to have to be happy at some point with how things look currently. When someone asks you if you're happy with how things are, answer them with, "Yes, happy about our progress. Happy but not content."

Really, if you come back to the question with anything along the lines of, "Yeah, it's done, and I'm awesome", then you're an idiot, and your venture is now on the decline.

All jokes aside, if you truly want to enjoy the satisfaction of accomplishment, you're going to have to adopt the work-in-progress mindset. And you *do* deserve it.

###

APPENDIX

BRYAN'S FAVORITE BOOKS

Shoe Dog, Phil Knight

Start with Why, Simon Sinek

Anything You Want, Derek Sivers

Let My People Go Surfing, Yvon Chouinard

Tools for Titans, Tim Ferris (Not just the Preface, but that's a good place to start)

Bryan's Playlist on Repeat

NPR: *How I Built This*

The Essential Lou Reed

###

THANK YOU

THANK YOU TO MY amazing wife and best friend, Emily. I couldn't do anything without you. In fact, without you in my life, I would be face down in the gutter, probably with chlamydia. I love you today. And the rest of the days, too.

Thanks to Jim at Epic Builders, John Comunale, and Josh Heiney, John Livaditis, Neil Cyrus, Kyle Messmer, Kevin, Uncle Dick, Dan Cox, the incredible editor Kathryn Galán, and all my friends and family.

Special thanks to Allie and Mel and the staff, for holding me accountable and making Easy Float great. Thanks to the best members on the planet: thank you for being Easy Float.

Thank you more than ever to the jerks who provided all of those sweet, sweet *NOs*... You know who you are, jerkoffs.

###

ABOUT BRYAN

BRYAN MESSMER is an entrepreneur who lives in Bend, Oregon with his wife and son. He founded Easy Float in Denver in February 2017. Bryan began writing books because he's a narcissist. He enjoys snowboarding with his wife, spending time with his son, fly fishing, drinking beers, and writing about himself in the third person.

###

55876541R00109

Made in the USA
Middletown, DE
18 July 2019